The Heretic

A play in three acts
by

Morris West

Heinemann London

Heinemann Educational Books Ltd
LONDON   EDINBURGH   MELBOURNE
SINGAPORE   JOHANNESBURG
IBADAN   HONG KONG
TORONTO   AUCKLAND
NEW DELHI   NAIROBI

ISBN 0 435 23930 9

Published by
Heinemann Educational Books Ltd
48 Charles Street, London W1X 8AH
Printed in Great Britain by
Cox & Wyman Ltd, London, Fakenham and Reading

16342

The Heretic

PREFACE

In the Campo dei Fiori, in Rome, stands the bronze statue of a man. His name: Giordano Bruno. The inscription indicates that the statue was raised in 1889, on the spot where Bruno was burned alive for heresy some 290 years earlier. It is recorded that on the day the statue was unveiled thirty thousand people gathered in the square to pay homage, and that the Pope, Leo XIII, fasted and issued a pastoral letter condemning both the commemoration and the man commemorated.

This play is about the trial and death of Giordano Bruno, a heretic.

The writing of an historical play is not the same thing as the writing of history. Both start with the collecting of facts, the gathering of information. Both require the use of intellect and imagination. But their purposes are different.

The historian is concerned with reconstructing what happened, the how and the why. Truth for him is the most accurate explanation and reconstruction possible after taking all the available evidence into account.

The playwright starts with the same body of facts, but he regards them with a different eye. He is not so much concerned with following the strict course of events as with the truths of personality. It is the people involved in history and their motives which fascinate him.

He concerns himself with imaginative reconstruction in order to get at the psychological truth. And in doing so, he may choose to modify a minor event of history in order more effectively to emphasize the major truth. He is also concerned with the making of moral judgements.

This play is solidly founded on historical documents. The Barber in the last act is recorded in the surviving extracts of the Roman process.

The story of the play is brutally simple. Giordano Bruno, a heretic in the eyes of his Church, is betrayed, tortured, and forced, in Venice, to go down on his knees to recant his errors. He thinks that by doing so he will save both his life and some part of his life's work.

But Bruno is a character too well known to get off lightly. The Inquisition must make a notable example of him. He is branded an heresiarch – that is to say, not only a heretic but the leader of a sect of heretics. He is transferred to Rome, over the objections of Venice and is kept in prison for seven years under constant pressure and interrogation. Finally he is presented with eight propositions drawn from his work by the Jesuit Cardinal, Robert Bellarmino. It is demanded that he recant these. He refuses and is burned alive in the Campo dei Fiori.

Why did Bruno refuse the second recantation? After the first it should have been easy for him. This is the truth at which the Author wishes to arrive in the play. He sees Bruno as a tragic figure confronted with a brutal choice: if he agrees to recant he loses his personal integrity and identity; if he does not he will be executed.

Bruno's dilemma is the dilemma of modern man. He cannot hope to beat the complex control mechanisms of the modern state, which, more and more, demands orthodoxy as the price of survival. He can never guarantee that he is right, he can only insist on his right to be wrong.

MORRIS WEST

ACKNOWLEDGEMENTS

The research for this play was prepared and collated by my son, Julian West, and is based upon the following works:

McIntyre, J. L., *Giordano Bruno* (Macmillan, 1963)

Singer, D. W., *Giordano Bruno: His Life And Thoughts* (Schumann, 1950)

Yates, F. A., *Giordano Bruno and the Hermetic Tradition* (Routledge, 1964)

Spampanato, V. (ed.), *Documenti Della Vita Di Giordano Bruno* (Florence, 1933)

Firpo, L., *Il Processo Di Giordano Bruno* (Naples, 1933)

Mercati, A. (ed.), *Il Sommario Del Processo Di Giordano Bruno* (Città del Vaticano, 1942)

Horowitz, I. L., *The Renaissance Philosophy of Giordano Bruno* (Coleman-Ross, 1952)

Nelson, J. C., *Renaissance Theory of Love* (Columbia U.P. 1958)

Giordano Bruno, *The Expulsion of the Triumphant Beast,* Tr. by Imerti, A.D. (Rutgers University Press, 1964)

Giordano Bruno, *Cause, Principle and Unity*, Tr. Lindsay, J. (International Pub. 1962)

Giordano Bruno, 'On The Infinite Universe and Worlds', Tr. Singer, D. W. (In *Giordano Bruno: His Life and Thoughts*)

Articles in the following encyclopaedias: Britannica, Colliers, Catholic.

The responsibility for the characterizations and inventions in this play is that of the Author.

NOTES ON CHARACTERS AND
THEIR FUNCTIONS

GIORDANO BRUNO, Dominican scholar, fugitive monk, convicted heretic. By nature, Bruno was short-tempered, irascible, and impatient of fools. A prodigious talker, boastful, at times vulgar and coarse in manner, he was possessed of great charm and intelligence.

He could not accommodate himself in the rigid and suspicious orthodoxy of the post-Trentine church. He desired an intellectual freedom impossible for the time in which he lived.

The Bruno of the play is faithful to the historical character – warts and all.

He is both hero and anti-hero. Comedian and tragic figure.

GIOVANNI MOCENIGO, a Venetian nobleman, 34 years old in 1592. Historically a member of one of the great Venetian mercantile families, and the man who invited Bruno to come to Venice and who then betrayed him to the Inquisition.

A spoiled and wilful man, he is interested in Bruno only because he sees in the philosopher's works the promise of personal power.

In the play he is shown to be self-centred, sexually frustrated, hungry for power which other members of his family have attained as Doges, Admirals, and Statesmen.

His handing over of Bruno to the Inquisition is an act calculated to give him the support of Rome in his political intrigues.

BORTOLO, Mocenigo's servant and household spy. Sly when unopposed, his slyness turns to fear and he becomes a comic figure when he encounters opposition.

PRIOR GABRIELLI, a Dominican, member of Bruno's own order of Friars Preachers, and Father Inquisitor to the Venetian Republic.

In the play he is Mocenigo's confessor and part of the plot to hand Bruno over to the Inquisitors.

Fundamentally he is a fair minded man. He dislikes and actively opposes the use of torture.

During the course of Bruno's trials and imprisonment, Gabrielli develops in stature, trying to understand Bruno's attitudes. But for all his fairmindedness and the friendship which grows up between the two men, Gabrielli remains trapped by his own orthodoxy.

LUDOVICO TAVERNA, Papal Nuncio to the Venetian Republic. Convinced of his own righteousness and that of his Church, Taverna is willing to achieve his ends by any means.

He is cold and ruthless, lacking in humanity.

He sees Bruno as two things: a pawn in the political game, and a threat to orthodoxy who must be made to recant his heresies.

A Machiavellian figure, he personifies the inhumanity of the Church as it struggles for reunion after the Reformation.

It is Taverna who insists on putting Bruno to the torture.

DONA DARIA, Mocenigo's wife. She has made an unhappy marriage, and turned to religion for solace.

She is afraid of Bruno at first because of his reputation, then attracted to him because of his adventurous and uncompromising spirit.

To protect Bruno from further pain she tries to persuade him to recant. The irony is that her love of Bruno betrays him into recantation.

TOMMASSO MOROSINI, the Civil member of the Venetian tribunal, he functions as the Assessor who has the right to intervene or to suspend the proceedings on behalf of the Venetian Republic.

Like Mocenigo, he belongs to a great Venetian mercantile family. Between the two families there is a rivalry for power in the Republic which is shown in the play in the clash between Mocenigo and Morosini.

He is a cynic, willing, so long as the ceremonies of diplomacy are observed, to hand Bruno over to the torturers.

He is canny and subtle.

He comes to admire Bruno and attempts, by persuading him to recant, to save Bruno's life. But his subtlety is outmatched by the ruthlessness of Taverna.

THE BARBER of the Roman prison. He is the perennial simple and honest man, sympathetic and friendly towards Bruno.

It is the kindness and respect which the Barber gives to Bruno that give him part of the courage to make his final stand.

In the play he is written for comedy and for pathos.

LAURENTIO PRIOLI, Patriarch of Venice. An ageing man, humane, who finds himself unable to control the events in which he is embroiled.

A NOTE ON PRONUNCIATION

There are large regional differences in Italian spelling and pronunciation. For the purposes of this text we have standardized the pronunciation as follows:

MOCENIGO	Mo-chen-EE-goh
BORTOLO	Bor-TOH-loh
DARIA	DAH-ree-ah
TAVERNA	Tah-VER-nah
MOROSINI	Moh-roh-SEE-nee
PRIOLI	Pree-OH-lee
GABRIELLI	Gah-bree-ELL-ee
CIOTTO	CHO-ttoh
FALIERI	Fal-YEH-ree
CONTARINI	Con-tah-REE-nee
ALVISE	Ahl-VEE-zay
ALDOBRANDINI	Ahl-doh-brahn-DEE-nee
TEOFILO IL VAIRANO	Tay-OFF-ee-loh/ il/ Vye-RAH-noh
VINCENZO COLLE IL SARNESE	Vin-CHEN-soh/ COH-lay/ il/ Sahr-NAY-zee

Much have I struggled. I thought I would be able to conquer . . .
And both fate and nature repressed my zeal and my strength.
Even to have come forth is something, since I see that being
    able to conquer
Is placed in the hands of fate. However, there was in me
Whatever I was able to do, that which no future century
Will deny to be mine, that which a victor could have for his own:
Not to have feared to die, not to have yielded to any equal
In firmness of nature, and to have preferred a courageous death to
A noncombatant life.

Giordano Bruno, *De Monade*

CAST

GIORDANO BRUNO, *A wandering scholar*
PRIOR GABRIELLI, *Inquisitor-General of Venice*
GIOVANNI MOCENIGO, *A Venetian Nobleman*
DONA DARIA, *Mocenigo's wife*
LUDOVICO TAVERNA, *Papal Nuncio to the Venetian Republic*
TOMMASSO MOROSINI, *Assessor of the Venetian Republic*
BORTOLO, *Mocenigo's Servant*
LAURENTIO PRIOLI, *The Patriarch of Venice*
A RECORDER, *of the Venetian Inquisition*
A BARBER, *of the Roman Inquisition*
A GAOLER, *of the Roman Inquisition*
A NOTARY, *of the Roman Inquisition*
CURIAL OFFICIALS, GUARDS, GAOLERS, etc.

The time: 1592–1600
The place: Venice and Rome

The Heretic

ACT ONE

SCENE ONE

Venice, 1591. *The library of the palace of Giovanni Mocenigo, scion of a family which to this date has produced a number of doges, a great admiral and many statesmen. A gallery runs across the rear of the room, and a staircase leads down to the stage level. There is one entrance from the gallery and another at the rear of the room. There is a large fireplace, over which hangs the portrait of the last Mocenigo Doge, Alvise III. There is a window alcove from which one looks down upon the traffic of the Grand Canal. The casement is open to the sunset glow. The sound of the city drifts in: the cries of the pedlars, the chant of the gondoliers, laughter, the shouts of revellers, a motley of music, the growl of approaching thunder.*

GIOVANNI MOCENIGO *stands in the alcove, looking down at the spectacle. He is a man in his mid-thirties, tall, lean, tormented. He turns abruptly with a gesture of disgust.*

MOCENIGO: Venice! A stinking city!
Dabbling like a duck in its own ordure,
Pecking at fruit-rinds, cabbage-stalks and turds,
Ripe-rotten peaches, fish-heads, turnip tops,
Dead cats and sodden bread and bloated meat,
Slops from the whore-house windows – Venice!
    He crosses to the table on which is set an ornate carafe of wine and jewelled goblets. He pours wine and makes an ironic toast to the portrait of the Doge Alvise.
MOCENIGO: To your city, Uncle!
    He drinks, draining the cup. The storm bursts in a clap of thunder

*and a gust of wind that slams the casements. He hurries to lock them
and draw the curtains.*

Bortolo! Lights! God's blood! Where are you, man?

    BORTOLO, *an elderly servant, hurries in with a taper and lights
the candles.* MOCENIGO *pours more wine and drinks compulsively.
The storm rises outside.*

BORTOLO: That should slack their lute strings!
  Wash off some patches, send some gallants home
  With sopping breeches!

MOCENIGO: Gallants! My God! The Turks
  Are creeping back. Spain and the Austrians snap
  About our flanks.... Where is our reverend counsellor, the Prior?
  And they make love-play!

BORTOLO (*a double-edged gesture*): With Dona Daria!

MOCENIGO: There's a clever one!
  Secret as the grave, suave as silk.
  A prayer book for my wife. For me a prod,
  A tiny dagger prick to say – 'Where Peter is,
  There is the Church. And where the Church,
  There are the dogs of God, to sniff out heresy,
  Confound the over-wise, bring down the high
  – Who, out of favour with the Ten, have yet
  No friends in Rome . . . ' (*A note of menace.*) I trust you, my
    Bortolo.

BORTOLO: I am deaf, my Lord.

MOCENIGO: And will be dumb, if you
  Breathe but a word of what you do not hear.

BORTOLO: Supper, my Lord?

MOCENIGO: I wait a guest.

BORTOLO: The storm
  Will hold him.

MOCENIGO (*laughs*): No! He needs the meal, the bed,
  A friend. These scholars are a hungry lot.
  This one a little hungrier than most,
  Therefore the more serviceable. Dona Daria

Must be prayed out. Entreat the worthy prior
To give her a special blessing and join me here.
BORTOLO: My Lord! . . .

He exits. MOCENIGO *crosses to the picture of his uncle and
stands facing it.*
MOCENIGO: Where are you now, Uncle? In heaven?
Or a private gilded hell for Doges
And the Decimal Councillors of this
Our Most Serene Republic? Where? I would like
To know. Up there? It would be blasphemy
To spit in your angelic eye and say,
'You lost us Nicosia, Famagusta,
And to me you lost all hope of eminence,
All favour of my peers.' Down there? Better!
I could with a little magic – which I hope
To learn! – summon you up on summer evenings,
Let you stroll, invisible of course,
Among the whores in the Piazza, breathe
For a little while the cool from the lagoon,
Savour the sunset splendour, hear the chink
Of honest gold among the changers' booths . . .
The sighs of lovers in the gondolas –
And then? A foot in your face to thrust you back
Into the sulphur; an ear cupped to hear
You sizzle in the frypan, crying: 'Giovanni!
Nephew Giovanni! Save me!' I would not
To save myself, save you, old man, one twitch
Of an eternity of dolours! Do you know
What you have done?

At this moment, PRIOR GABRIELLI, *the Domenican, enters and
stands listening.*
You have castrated me!
Made me a chirping cantor in the choir
When, once I might have shouted down Saint Marks,
And set the lions trembling on their pedestals.

PRIOR GABRIELLI: You could again, my Lord . . . !
  MOCENIGO *whirls to face him.*
MOCENIGO: You intrude, Prior!
PRIOR GABRIELLI *(calm)*: No! I was called. I came. The bruised
    spirit
  Cries out in torment. I am fortunate
  To hear the cry – a confessional confidence,
  Believe me! – I am a doctor of sick souls,
  I dispense the soothing balm of faith
  And hope and Christian charity.
    MOCENIGO, *recovering himself, crosses to the wine flagon.*
MOCENIGO: Wine?
PRIOR GABRIELLI: A small cup – for the stomach's sake!
    MOCENIGO *pours wine and hands him the cup.*
PRIOR GABRIELLI: To peace
  In the house of Mocenigo!
MOCENIGO: I count on you
  To bring it, Prior.
    They drink.
  My wife is chastely shriven?
PRIOR GABRIELLI: Your wife is a noble spirit, purified
  By daily sacraments, by prayer, good works
  – And by a singular forbearance! Virtue
  Goes out from her.
MOCENIGO: God's blood! And how it goes!
  And goes and goes!
PRIOR GABRIELLI: Do you wish to confess?
MOCENIGO: Not yet! I need a preparation. Time
  To fill up a tally of more manly sins
  Before I kneel in penitence.
PRIOR GABRIELLI: My Lord,
  There is no guarantee of time. Our God
  Is not a banker signing notes of credit
  Upon our promises.
MOCENIGO *(cheerful again)*: Well said, good Prior!

On the other hand, God does make bargains
With his chosen ones. God's Vicar, he
Who sits in Rome on Peter's throne and wears
The ring of Peter – he makes bargains, too.
He binds, he loosens, he lifts up, puts down.
He is the servant, is he not, of those
Who serve God's cause.

PRIOR GABRIELLI: It is his proudest title.

MOCENIGO: So! We can bargain. You for him. And I
For restoration of my house and name
To a high office in the Serenissima
– The Doge's cap, perhaps, or better yet,
A seat in the High Council of the Ten.
Think on that, Prior!

PRIOR GABRIELLI: I am thinking.
I ask how Rome can speak in the cabals
Of Venice.

MOCENIGO: She can. Red hats and bishoprics,
Abbacies, Priories – These are tongues of fire!

PRIOR GABRIELLI: I ask then what could Mocenigo do
That others could not, would not, for the Pope.

MOCENIGO: What others? Number them on your sacred hands.
Spell out their names – Falieri, Contarini,
All the rest. Will they give Rome one ship,
One gun, one man, one ducat for defence
Against the Turks? Will they denounce a Switzer
Calvanist, a Lutheran from Mainz,
A vile Waldensian, an English lord
Reeking of heresy and tobacco smoke,
– So long as they have trade to make – Never!

PRIOR GABRIELLI (*dry*): But a Mocenigo would be different?

MOCENIGO: A grateful Mocenigo. Yes.

PRIOR GABRIELLI: My lord,
I am your friend and I believe you – but
In Rome they believe only in God.

MOCENIGO: And He,
  To make them so believe, rose from the dead.
PRIOR GABRIELLI (*laughs*): Can you do that?
MOCENIGO (*savage*): Rise from the dead? No!
  But out of this limbo, yes!
PRIOR GABRIELLI: Without Rome?
MOCENIGO: With or without! You choose!
PRIOR GABRIELLI (*a fear*): Make me an offer,
  Give me one gift in hand that says to Rome
  'Giovanni Mocenigo is a man
  Of power and possibility for the Church.
  Lift him and Rome is lifted – one fulcrum
  For a double hoist . . . '
MOCENIGO (*satisfied at last*): Good! Now, tell me, Prior,
  What is Rome's greatest fear? What gives the Pope
  More night-mares than bad sausage?
PRIOR GABRIELLI: Heresy!
  The rending of the seamless robe of truth.
  This rabble of mountebanks and maguses
  Who shout reform, defile the Eucharist,
  Flout all authority, elect false bishops,
  Deny the Trinity and saving grace,
  Abolish marriage, set their private minds
  Against the long tradition of the Faith
  And Peter's dictates and the Holy Writ . . .
MOCENIGO: But they flourish, Prior. Why?
PRIOR GABRIELLI: They are a plague,
  A dancing madness!
MOCENIGO: People like to dance.
PRIOR GABRIELLI: And every Prince would like to be Pope,
  And every clown a Plato!
MOCENIGO: So, the cure?
PRIOR GABRIELLI: Obedience in humble faith.
MOCENIGO: Enforced
  By Whom?

PRIOR GABRIELLI: Induced by prayer.
MOCENIGO: They pray in Zurich,
   But against the Pope.
PRIOR GABRIELLI: That is a blasphemy,
   And blasphemy is criminal. A Christian prince
   Must rule for God, from whom his power flows.
   He must burn out impurities with fire,
   Rack, rend and quite destroy God's enemies.
MOCENIGO: There is your gift in hand, Prior. Myself!
   A hammer against heresy! But not,
   As I am now, hung on the smithy wall
   For want of arms to swing me! A bargain, yes?
PRIOR GABRIELLI: I cannot bargain for the Pope. I can
   Provide a prelude . . .
MOCENIGO (*eagerly comic*): Well composed? Sweet strings
      of lutes? Viols and mandolas? Fiddlers,
   Tambourines and flutes?
PRIOR GABRIELLI: If you can pay,
   My lord – a choir of angels!
MOCENIGO (*following the paranoic comedy*): Name the price!
   A fresco for your Priory? Tintoretto's old
   But good – God's blood, he's good! – An altarcloth
      of pearls? A mass-cup, gold on crysoprase?
   Titles of land in perpetuity?
   Name it!
PRIOR GABRIELLI (*carefully*): A caution here! The gifts of
      piety,
   Are rich in merit. But from Prince to Pope,
   What is another jewel more or less,
   Another pumpkin patch? The offering
   Should speak a thousand words by silence, show
   Heart's reasons at a glance, and make a pact,
   In secret that no notary could frame,
   No prudent prince could ratify.
   You take my meaning?

MOCENIGO: I do. And I am grateful.
I will think on it.

> BORTOLO *enters with an announcement.*

BORTOLO: Your guest, my Lord.

MOCENIGO: Hold him a moment.

> BORTOLO *exits.*

Prior, my respects.
And though you do not ask it. Tintoretto
Will have your fresco in a twelvemonth.

PRIOR GABRIELLI: And the Pope, my prelude, sooner.

MOCENIGO: Bless me, Father.

> *He bows his head. The* PRIOR *signs his brow with his thumb.*

PRIOR GABRIELLI: May the blessing of the Lord Omnipotent
Descend upon you and remain forever.

MOCENIGO: Amen! . . . Bortolo! Present our guest!

> BORTOLO *enters and bows the guest into the room.* GIORDANO
> BRUNO *enters. He is a man of forty-three, more ugly than hand-*
> *some. He is dressed in a long, hooded cloak over clothes which have*
> *seen better days. He is eager, cheerful, shrewd, assertive. He is*
> *sensitive to slights, too apt to boast. He lacks discretion and social*
> *subtlety.*

BORTOLO: My Lords,
The scholar Giordano Bruno.

> BRUNO *bows.*

MOCENIGO: Welcome, sir!

BRUNO: What a night! Every road's a bog! Each lane
A cataract!

MOCENIGO (*a note of distaste*): This is the Prior Gabrielli,
Inquisitor General of the Serenissima!

BRUNO (*cheerful*): My honour! You are my first inquisitor!
The last, I hope!

> *The joke falls flat. The* PRIOR *studies Bruno groping for a recol-*
> *lection.*

PRIOR GABRIELLI: Bruno . . . your given name?

BRUNO: My only one, sir.

PRIOR GABRIELLI: Where were you born?

BRUNO: Nola.

PRIOR GABRIELLI: I caught the accent of the South . . . an echo,
  too,
  Out of our case-books. There was a certain friar
  Of my own Order of Preachers, a fugitive
  From vows, a vagabond philosopher.
  He taught – now let me see – Paris and Oxford,
  Prague and Wittenburg, Helmstedt and Zurich.
  He was in prison there, I think. He wrote
  An obscene comedy, some suspect treatises.
  A work on memory, dialogues – his name . . .

BRUNO (*curt*): Giordano Bruno. I am he.

  The PRIOR *casts an inquiring glance at Mocenigo. His silence is an*
  irony.

PRIOR GABRIELLI: You are bold!
  With your case open still, to put yourself
  So close in reach of Rome and her pursuivants.

BRUNO: No, sir. I trust the justice of my cause,
  The charity of Mother Church, the noble house
  Which lends me patronage.

PRIOR GABRIELLI: You will remember,
  You have no licence to teach publicly,
  Nor preach in church nor give the sacraments.

BRUNO: I do not seek it, sir.

MOCENIGO: I am his surety.

  The PRIOR *bows and moves to the door with* MONCENIGO.
  They ignore Bruno.
  Our bargain then is clear. You will write
  With urgency to our high personage . . .

  They exit. BRUNO *slips off his cloak.* BORTOLO *takes it. He*
  points to the sword-belt. BRUNO *unbuckles it, chuckling.*

BRUNO: Within these friendly walls, no further need.

  BORTOLO *exits.* BRUNO *relaxes, taking in his surroundings. He*
  catches sight of the wine, he pours himself a long draught and drinks

with satisfaction. He sets down the glass and then begins to walk about the room, fingering its treasures. He is playing a comedy of self-mockery, the fortunate oaf who has found a feather bed. He pauses by an ornate mirror and jibes at his own reflection, sticking out his tongue, making faces as a child does.

BRUNO: Oh Brother Bruno! What a clod you are!
You talk, talk, talk, talk, talk! –
A very parakeet without the plumes.
You make jokes with the Grand Inquisitor,
Him with the thumbscrew in his pocket – Bah!
I lose all patience with you – Raggedy Jack.
Empty of purse and belly, patched and darned,
Down to your last shoe leather – yet you strut
Like Socrates before he heard of hemlock!
Brother, little brother, mend your manners!
Tie your tongue: This is a dangerous city
For a babbler. Here they denounce you with a note
Unsigned, slipped in a lion's mouth, and then
One fine spring day, you're hanging by the heels
In the Piazza, dead as mutton!

There is a sound of voices outside. He composes himself instantly, picks up a book from the table and assumes a studious pose MOCEN-IGO *enters, with* BORTOLO *in attendance.* MOCENIGO *surveys his guest with ironic amusement.*

MOCENIGO: So! Master Bruno!
BRUNO: My Lord?
MOCENIGO: You need new clothes!
BRUNO (*wry*): In truth I do!
MOCENIGO: A sober suiting, mind!
Scholarly, discreet. You bathe, I trust?
BRUNO: When I have money for the scrub-house, yes.
MOCENIGO: My steward pays your stipend by the month,
You may draw modestly against it.
Are you poxed?
You have

   No sickness of the lungs, infectious tumours?

BRUNO: None.

MOCENIGO: Do you drink?

BRUNO: Cheerfully.

MOCENIGO: No tavern brawls!
   No tangles with the watch! The Mocenigo
   Have a name to keep.

BRUNO: And I, my lord,
   Have certain monkish ways to which I hold.

MOCENIGO: How much a monk, eh? I am tolerant
   Of private peccadilloes,
   But I want
   No swollen bellies on my servant-girls,
   Play outside, eh?

     BRUNO *is silent.* MOCENIGO *is momentarily out of countenance.*
   He goes on, more respectfully.

MOCENIGO: From first collation
   Until noon you are at call, and then
   From sunset until supper. If you walk abroad.
   My messengers must know how to recall you
   In an hour. You will tell no man – or woman –
   The secrets that we share. You do have secrets,
   Yes? Disciplines of power? Hidden arts?

BRUNO (*grins*): None that bear telling on an empty stomach.

     MOCENIGO *snaps his fingers at Bortolo.*

MOCENIGO: Bortolo! Supper for Master Bruno!

BORTOLO: My Lord!

     BORTOLO *exits.* MOCENIGO *becomes eager and secretive.*

MOCENIGO: Now, Master Bruno, let us say it plain.
   You are a magician!

     BRUNO *laughs and dodges a direct answer.*

BRUNO: You, my Lord
   Have said it; but I do not admit the charge.
   Why come to Venice to write my death warrant?

     MOCENIGO *laughs, too.*

MOCENIGO: Well answered! But the Inquisitor is gone,
And we are secret here as hermits in a desert.
You have the formularies of the Jews?
You know the Cabbala? The secret names?
The invocations of Beelzebub,
The magic squares, the spells, the pentagram?
You practise alchemy? You can concoct
Love potions – and dispel the evil eye?

BRUNO (*hedging*): And if I could, my Lord?

MOCENIGO: Make me an adept, too!

BRUNO: To what end?

MOCENIGO: To enrich yourself.

BRUNO (*an irony*): Such base
And mercenary use of the great powers
Entails a manifold damnation.

MOCENIGO: For me then!
Mocenigo is bent upon high enterprise.
Put power into his hands, and you have power
Beyond your dreaming. Be my tutor now
In magic arts and you will be my Chamberlain,
Heart's favourite, beyond the touch of Rome,
The ten, the whimsical malice of any man.
What say you, Master?

    BRUNO *is now in a dilemma. If he confesses that he is not a magician, Mocenigo may reject him. If he admits to magical power, he must make good the claim. He does not answer immediately. He hesitates, reflects and answers with sober conviction.*

BRUNO: My Lord, the things you ask,
I could engage to teach you. Give me vials,
Liquors and alembics, copper and lead,
A cellar to make the stinks in, I could be
The most proliferous alchemist in Europe.
But gold from lead? No man has done it, nor can.
Magic? Give me chalk and compasses,
A cat for my familiar, mouldy books

Written in a gibberish, I'll make the hairs stand up
On a clerk's tonsure! This is mummery
And humbug!

   MOCENIGO *now begins to show resentment and suspicion. He takes his jewelled dagger from its sheath and begins to whet the blade upon his thumb. His tone is sullen and insulting.*

MOCENIGO: I am told otherwise by your betters!
BRUNO (*snaps back*): Betters or no, these are carnival tricks
   For knaves to practise, fools to tremble at.
MOCENIGO (*anger*): Tell me straight. Can you make incantations,
   Spells?
BRUNO: I can! And so can you!
MOCENIGO: How?
BRUNO: Walk
   In town, look solemn, puffed with portents! Start
   A whisper about any man – premise his death,
   A looseness in his wife, a treachery
   Of friends. Within a day, he's cringing from the prick
   Of unseen daggers, fasting for fear of poison
   In the wine-cup. My Lord, what else is magic.

   MOCENIGO *approaches him. There is the hint of madness in his face. He presses the dagger-point to Bruno's breast.*

MOCENIGO: So tell me, Master Bruno. On your life
   – This shabby and uncertain little span! –
   Why should I feed you, clothe you, keep you safe
   From the white hounds of God, pay you good gold,
   To teach me what I know already?

   BRUNO *is very cool. He has to be.*

BRUNO: You should not!
   Nor should you blame me, sir, because I will not cheat
   To save my shabby self.
MOCENIGO (*uncertain now*): What have you then
   For me, who pay the score?
BRUNO (*blunt*): A lifetime's learning!
   Little or much it's all the wealth I own . . .

BORTOLO enters, carrying a supper tray. He sets it down on the table.

BORTOLO: The scholar's supper!

MOCENIGO relaxes and sheaths his dagger. His smile is a threat.

MOCENIGO: You are snappish, sir!

I hope to find you blander in the morning.

Good appetite!

He exits. BRUNO *looks after him, frowning. Then he shrugs and turns to the meal. He does not sit, but inspects the meagre fare with distaste.*

BRUNO: This is a supper?

BORTOLO (*veiled insult*): Have you

Eaten better?

BRUNO (*anger*): And in nobler houses!

He takes BORTOLO by the neck and forces him into the chair. He pushes his face down into the platter.

BRUNO: Go on! Look at it man! Taste it! Smell it!

Corpse-cold! Too rank even for a beggar's belly.

Did your master order this? Or did you dream it

As a love-feast for Brother Bruno? Answer me!

BORTOLO: I – I carried what was served –

BRUNO hoists him to his feet and thrusts the tray into his hands.

BRUNO: Then carry it back!

Tell them in the kitchen, I will eat

A bowl of soup, a roast of chicken, cheese,

A pear with grapes. – And send me honest wine,

Not vinegar.

BORTOLO: I will order it.

BRUNO will not let him go, but twists his ear between thumb and forefinger. BORTOLO *writhes unhappily.*

BRUNO: Bortolo?

BORTOLO: Sir?

BRUNO: A scholar is no butt for oafs.

BORTOLO: No, sir.

BRUNO: He comes to teach your master wisdom.

BORTOLO: Yes, sir.

BRUNO: And you a mannerly service!

BORTOLO: Yes, sir.

BRUNO: You will not keep me standing while you stuff
Your own belly in the kitchen, will you?

BORTOLO: No, sir.
My oath on that!

BRUNO: Swear for the cook, too.

BORTOLO: I swear.

BRUNO: And for the scullery maids.

BORTOLO: I swear!

BRUNO: I am hungry. Go!

BRUNO *releases him and he trots out dolefully.* BRUNO *chuckles.*
He pours wine from Mocenigo's flagon and carries it over to the
casement. He draws back the curtains and throws open the window.
The summer storm is over, there is a moonlight and the sound of
distant singing over the renewed rumour of the city. BRUNO *sits in*
the alcove and relaxes into weariness.

DONA DARIA *enters. She is a sad but stately beauty in her late*
twenties. She is carrying a book. She catches sight of Bruno, who is
absorbed in the outside spectacle. Her first greeting is cool.

DONA DARIA: Are you the scholar?

BRUNO *is startled. He turns and gets awkwardly to his feet.*

BRUNO: My Lady?

DONA DARIA: Are you the scholar Bruno?

BRUNO: Yes.

DONA DARIA: I am the wife of Mocenigo.

BRUNO (*bows*): Madam.

DONA DARIA: You are not welcome here!

BRUNO: So I have found, my Lady.

DONA DARIA (*taken aback*): My husband says
You are a notable heretic, a master
Of black arts.

BRUNO: Neither, madam.

DONA DARIA: My husband –

BRUNO (*grins*): Hoped for a trout, my lady, caught a catfish,
   And is less pleased than you to have me here.

DONA DARIA: Why stay, then? Have you no pride?

BRUNO: O, pride a plenty!
   But no money. Therefore no liberty,
   Except to starve or – cheerful thought – to sell
   Myself as galley rower at the docks,
   Even for that I lack the muscle!

DONA DARIA: How comes
   A man of brains to such a sorry pass?

BRUNO: Good question, madam! Why are we what we are?
   I've gnawed at that dry bone for twenty years,
   There's no meat left on it. The Mussulman
   Comes closest to the answer. Our destiny
   Is written on our palms; a bawdy joke,
   The graffito of God we lack the wit
   To read.

DONA DARIA: That is a blasphemy!

BRUNO (*exasperated*): Is it?
   Then read my hand and make a psalm instead!
      *There is a moment of silence as she stares at his out-thrust
   hand, and then at his tight, angry face. Into the silence comes a
   song from a young male voice outside the window.* DONA DARIA
   softens.

DONA DARIA: I beg your pardon, sir. I have no right
   To plague you.

BRUNO (*relaxes*): I plague myself. Pebble-in-shoe,
   Burrs-in-breeches Bruno! (*He adverts to the music.*) What does he
      sing?

DONA DARIA (*follows beat*): 'Farfalla, farfalla, farfalla, vagante
   Leggera sei tu come la mia amante.'
   The butterfly song – it tells of fickle love!

BRUNO (*nostalgic irony*): Fickle or not, it would be sweet to
   taste . . .

DONA DARIA: And has the scholar Bruno never loved?
BRUNO: I have been merry with women, sad betimes,
  And solitary always in the morning.
DONA DARIA: Never a mistress?
BRUNO: Oh, yes!
DONA DARIA: Was she not kind?
BRUNO: Most cruel! Capricious as a folly-fire,
  Cold and secret as a Pharaoh's tomb,
  Then of a sudden – Hey! Ho! Halloo!
  A beat in the blood, a madness in the brain!
DONA DARIA: Where is she now?
BRUNO: Who knows?
DONA DARIA: What is her name?
BRUNO: Veritas . . .
DONA DARIA: The truth? You mock me, sir.
BRUNO: No, madam! There are a few of us – madmen all! –
  Who are in love with knowing, who would sell
  The last shirt from our backs, for one small truth,
  One tiny star-fire to light up the murk
  And mystery of what we call our life . . .
  We may go blind before we see it, that's
  The haunting –
    His mood changes as BORTOLO *enters with the new supper
    tray.*
BRUNO: Ah! Our ancient Ganymede!
    He makes a comical inspection of the tray.
BRUNO: Much better! A scholar's compliment to all
  Those sweating scullions. A platter for my lady?
DONA DARIA: No! This is my fasting day.
    BORTOLO *sets down the tray, pours wine and stands waiting.*
    BRUNO *seats himself ceremoniously, then waves Bortolo away.*
BRUNO: Go, friend, and sup
  In peace and charity.
    BORTOLO *exits.* BRUNO *picks up a chicken leg and studies
    it.*

C

BRUNO: A grace, madam.
  – For the unwelcome guest?
DONA DARIA: I bid you welcome!
  In the sweet name of God and in my own.
BRUNO (*sober*): I am thankful . . .
DONA DARIA: And hungry! Eat, sir, and enjoy!
    BRUNO *begins to eat ravenously.* DONA DARIA *relaxes and*
    seats herself at the table. BRUNO *talks between mouthfuls.*
BRUNO: Why do you fast, my lady?
DONA DARIA: A discipline!
BRUNO (*a note of mockery*): Hairshirt as well? Cold vigils?
    Knotted cords?
DONA DARIA (*sharp*): And if there were?
BRUNO: Why so misuse what God
  Has so munificently made?
DONA DARIA: Penance
  Is enjoined upon us all. A monk
  Should know that; even –
    She breaks off. BRUNO *completes the thought.*
BRUNO (*chuckles*): Such a monk as I?
  Madam, beware of celibates who first
  Renounce, and then desire, and then for shame,
  Most rigorously condemn what they do not
  Enjoy. This is a eunuch breed. For me,
  God made woman, a cushion for the world,
  Her lips a honeycomb, her breasts a spring
  Of sweetness, her hands a healing miracle,
  Her womb a harbourage of fragile life
  – Why would he then pronounce sentence of torment
  On his masterwork?
DONA DARIA (*a poignant revelation*): He did it, Bruno,
  Does it every day. The honeycomb
  Is empty and the spring dried up. The womb
  Is barren, nothing moves therein. No life,
  No giver of life, only a nightly hunger

That must be stilled before it turns to frenzy.

> BRUNO *pours wine and offers it to her with bread and cheese.*
> *He is very gentle now.*

BRUNO: Drink a little wine. Take this and eat.

DONA DARIA (*puzzled*): Why do you tempt me?

BRUNO: It was the last commandment
Of our Lord. Break bread in charity,
Two or three together. We are two,
It is enough to make an agape!

> DONA DARIA *begins to eat hesitantly, and then with enjoyment.*
> BRUNO *goes on with his meal.*

DONA DARIA: Why do they call you heretic?

BRUNO: Beh!
They need a cry to rally up the hounds
And set them baying after Brother Fox!

DONA DARIA: That's half an answer –

BRUNO: And the other half,
How stand I, measured by the creeds, tradition,
The writings of the Fathers, acts of all
The councils, Nice, Chalcedon, Trent?
I do not know. I do not greatly care.
No man – prince, peasant, pope – has all the light,
Who says else is a mountebank. I claim
No private lien on the truth, only
A liberty to seek it, prove it in debate,
And to be wrong a thousand times to reach
A single rightness. It is that liberty
They fear. They want us driven to God like sheep,
Not running to him like lovers, shouting joy!

DONA DARIA: But why?

BRUNO: Ever since the Greeks, we have been drunk
With language! We have made a cage of words
And showed our God inside, as boys confine
A cricket or a locust, to make him sing
A private song! And look what great gob-stopping

Words we use for God's simplicity,
Hypostasis and homoousion!
We burn men for these words – a baboon chatter
Of human ignorance! – We burn men!
DONA DARIA: For their purpose then, it is enough
To have you heretic. Why are you called
Magician?
BRUNO: They need hobgoblins, too – a fear
To hold the hunt together, so they eat,
Drink, sleep and breed, a single tribe,
Protective of itself, self-justified.
DONA DARIA: But are you not afraid?
BRUNO: Oh yes, I am!
I am Red Reynard, broken-winded, torn
Run down to rib-cage, scuttling to earth,
To lick his wounds, and get his courage up.
DONA DARIA: For what?
BRUNO: Another journey.
DONA DARIA: Where?
BRUNO: Home!
DONA DARIA: And where is home?
BRUNO: Oh, where is home? My lady,
You will laugh at my simplicity.
The quaint religion of a runaway.
Home is a convent, high on a Nolan hill,
Grey walls, a tired campanile that leans
Against blue sky, a cloister with white doves,
And orange-flowers and a sound of bells,
Vineyards that climb around the slopes,
Green fields, abundant in the summer sun,
The brethren picking beans and topping lettuces,
Skirts tucked into their cinctures, tonsures bare,
While the cicadas chant the matin song
Of Brother Sun!

He breaks off, caught in reverie. DONA DARIA *prompts him gently.*

DONA DARIA: And what of Brother Bruno?

BRUNO: He comes, flip-flop in sandals, up the road.
He's slow, stooped in the back, his footsoles ache,
He's older by a century than when
He walked out, whistling, to confront the world.
The brethren wait. They have been pilgrims, too.
They have a patience for the wanderer,
They know the grail-search must be made alone.
They will not chide the prodigal, nor question him,
Enough that he is home . . .

He lapses again, and then abruptly shatters the self-created illusion.

BRUNO: Oh God! What home?
What brethren? I am a leper with a bell
Around my neck! Because I cannot bend
To all their systems and their syllogisms!

He slams a fist on the table, heaves himself up and strides to the window, where he stands, tense and rigid, staring out at the traffic of the Grand Canal. DONA DARIA *stands too, moves a pace or two towards him, and then stops. She is now what Bruno has named her, the cushion of the world.*

DONA DARIA: Master Bruno!

BRUNO: Yes?

DONA DARIA: I am no judge of men.
I know – and him not well or happily –
Only the one I married. You are strange,
You take away the props that hold my faith.
You leave me shaken in a winter wind.
And yet . . .

BRUNO (*harsh*): Ignore me, madam! I am a lackey
Here!

Unseen by both, unnoticed by the audience, MOCENIGO *enters and stands in the gallery above.*

DONA DARIA: Yet, in a city full of pigs,
You stand up like a man!

MOCENIGO: Bravissimo!

They both turn, shocked and speechless. MOCENIGO *surveys them from above, like a puppet-master.*

MOCENIGO: A noble vindication! Master Bruno,
You must have a care to earn the praise
My wife bestows on you. – And you, dear lady,
Will you come to bed!

There is a frozen moment and then DONA DARIA *moves like an automaton up the stairs towards her husband.*

CURTAIN

The same. 1592. It is still winter in Venice. A log fire blazes in the
hearth. The curtains are drawn. Candles are lit.

BORTOLO *ushers in two visitors,* PRIOR GABRIELLI *and* LUDOVICO
  TAVERNA, *the Papal Nuncio. Both are cloaked and hooded*
  against the cold. PRIOR GABRIELLI *coughs asthmatically and talks*
  compulsively.

PRIOR GABRIELLI: This fog!
  A cobweb in the lungs! My bones protest
  Each God-forgotten winter on the lagoons!
    They take off their cloaks and hand them to Bortolo.
BORTOLO: My Master begs your patience, gentlemen.
    TAVERNA *chuckles and backs up gratefully to the fire.*
TAVERNA: Patience! Mine is worn thin around the backside!
  Spavined nags, cold comfort at the inns,
  Slush in the plains and snow in every pass
  From Rome to the Romagna! His Holiness
  Owes me a favour for this purgatory!
    BORTOLO *exits.*
PRIOR GABRIELLI: Good news from Venice and he may double
  it.
TAVERNA: Have we good news?
    PRIOR GABRIELLI *makes a cautious gesture and drops his voice.*
PRIOR GABRIELLI: Good dispositions here.
  But problems to be solved. Mocenigo
  Is ranged with Rome in secret, but must make
  For polity, a Venetian masquerade.
TAVERNA: That's a noble Christian!

PRIOR GABRIELLI (*wry shrug*): Our proverb says,
  'Venetians first and Christians afterwards!'
TAVERNA: I did not come, Sir Prior, to peddle proverbs!
  A new pontiff sits on Peter's throne,
  Christ's Vicar and my noble master Clement,
  Eighth of the name. His charge to me is this:
  'Find me a man who will hold Venice safe
  Against the heretics, restore the old
  Authority of Rome, the true respect,
  For Christ, His Vicar, and his hierarchy
  Find me that man, and pledge him our support,
  Our Apostolic love, our princely might
  Against the Church's enemies, and his!'
  In Mocenigo, have we found him? Yes –
  Or no?
PRIOR GABRIELLI: As far as I can read him, yes!
TAVERNA: How far is that?
PRIOR GABRIELLI (*a studious care*): Your Excellency knows
  Better than I, how power changes men.
  Ask me to guarantee against the change
  – I cannot. Nor can you. We ask and get
  A promise of performance, A and B
  And C and D, down to the final Zeta.
  Then we say, 'For our security
  And the good faith of Mocenigo, seal
  The bargain with a warranty.' Can we
  Do more? What do we risk?
TAVERNA: A treachery!
PRIOR GABRIELLI: And if we do not risk? Venice is still
  The Adriatic whore who'll sell herself
  To English protestant, Hussite or Zwinglian,
  – Yes, to a Muslim pirate – for their trade.

  TAVERNA *is still digesting this proposition when* MOCENIGO,
  accompanied by DONA DARIA, *enters from the gallery. He is
  cheerful and expansive.*

MOCENIGO: Forgive me, sirs! My lady held me late
   With a momentous matter, a seemly gown,
   A modesty of jewels in which to greet
   The Legate of His Holiness . . .
TAVERNA: My lady!
   From the hand of Peter, a benediction,
   From myself, a humble greeting.
DONA DARIA (*curtsies*): Sir!
   My thanks.
MOCENIGO: My house is yours. My life in service
   To the Holy See. Wine for our guests!
      They seat themselves as DONA DARIA *pours wine.* MOCENIGO
   talks on.
   Be comfortable! Firelight, fellowship,
   And private talk. No protocol! No hedge
   To what we say inside these walls! Your health!
      They drink. DONA DARIA *takes a book and retires discreetly to*
   the alcove.
PRIOR GABRIELLI: My Lord, the prelude has been played, and
      now
   The curtain's up, the opera begins!
MOCENIGO (*cheerfully*): Sing it to me, Prior! My ear is good.
   I promise not to miss a single grace-note,
   Glissando or cadenza.
PRIOR GABRIELLI: So! We treat
   Of sacred things, not politics!
MOCENIGO: Of course!
PRIOR GABRIELLI: Our noble pontiff, recently installed,
   Weeps nightly at the rifts in Christendom.
MOCENIGO: And we weep with him.
PRIOR GABRIELLI: But not all. In Venice
   In the sacred shadow of St. Mark,
   Lion of the Evangelists, we flirt
   With schism. Our Senate names our bishops, not
   The Pope! Our Patriarch – God give him light! –

Cannot convene a Synod, unless the Doge
First nods approval! We ballot for our priests
Like prizes in a lottery. We exclude
All but Venetian born – so that if Paul
Or Luke or Mark came back as ministers,
We must refuse them. In this the most Serene
And Catholic Republic, we are worse
Than English heretics, who make their King
– Their Queen, indeed! – a Pope. It must be changed!
The family of Christians must be one.
United in its Father's house!

MOCENIGO (*irony*): And I
Can bring them home?

TAVERNA: At least bring Venice back.
Out of Byzantium into the West.

    MOCENIGO *is too shrewd to be trapped into a facile promise. He
smiles and shakes his head.*

MOCENIGO: My friend – Believe me, I am more a friend
Than most in this fair city! – You must not ask
Impossibles! I must not claim to be
A thaumaturge who can make mountains walk!
How long was Rome a-building? Venice will not
Be made a virtuous woman overnight!

TAVERNA: How long, then?

MOCENIGO: How long to come to power? How long
To use the power – fit lever under stone
And set it rolling?

TAVERNA: Guess, then!

MOCENIGO: I will not!
Rather, I will show you – a risk to me,
But nonetheless an honesty I owe! –
What holds us anchored in Byzantium,
What makes our nobles jealous of privilege,
Our commons fractious, apt for novelty!

TAVERNA (*reluctant admiration*): You play boldly, sir.

MOCENIGO: The stakes are high,
  No less for Rome than me!
    He stands, dominating them. He is forceful and eloquent.
MOCENIGO: Let us be blunt.
  Forget the reverent hypocrisies!
  Remember Cambrai and the infamous league
  Of French and Spaniards and Hungarians,
  Led by Pope Julius – our spiritual father! –
  To destroy our most serene republic!
  We are mistrustful now! With reason! We ask,
  Do shepherds kill their sheep? Fathers their sons?
  I stand in our Great Council and I plead
  A catholic amity, familial love!
  They laugh me out of countenance! I beg
  A unity in faith, a resignation
  Of old privilege. They wag wise heads
  And tell me, 'Who goes to supper with the Pope,
  Takes a long spoon and keeps his sword arm free!'
  You know this, Prior. Your noble master, sir,
  Carries Pope Julius on his back, dead
  Though he be!
TAVERNA: He wants to get him off!
  He needs an advocate.
MOCENIGO: The advocate
  Needs time and subtlety, strong argument,
  To make his case. Not in the Council only,
  But with the people! They are restive now.
  They know what Luther did in Germany,
  They know that Rome is not impregnable,
  That her decrees are not – not always, sir! –
  Dictated by the Holy Spirit. So,
  There is for us a double jeopardy,
  The nobles and the commons!
TAVERNA: The commons are sheep!
  They can be led or driven!

MOCENIGO: Can they so?

At this moment, BRUNO's *voice is heard, singing, a little drunkenly,* 'Farfalla, farfalla'. *All turn at the sound. The* PRIOR *frowns,* DONA DARIA *looks worried.* MOCENIGO, *however, seizes the interruption to make his point.*

Here's my Bruno! Here is a man who knows
The people in their habits and habitats.
He is common born, less than discreet,
Uncommon studious, with a lively ear,
A loose tongue, a taste for disputation.
Let us hear him!

PRIOR GABRIELLI: I beg you, no, my Lord,
These are high matters —

TAVERNA: Let us hear him, Prior!

BRUNO *enters, still singing, and then breaks off in tipsy surprise.*

BRUNO: My Lords! My Lady! Forgive me! I have been
Abroad – no, not abroad. Settled felic –
Felicitously in a tavern, a place
For sailors on the Giudecca. There was a man,
A giant blackamoor, built like a barrel,
Baubles in his ears, a parrot red and green
Perched on his shoulder – A most eloquent bird!
Blasphemous, too! Spoke Greek and Arabic
Italian and High German. This blackamoor —

DONA DARIA *approaches and tries to draw him away.*

DONA DARIA: Master Bruno, my husband and these gentlemen
Discuss affairs of state . . .

BRUNO: Oh! then I'll go drink
A bowl of broth . . .

MOCENIGO: No! No! Sit with us!
We need a scholar's perspicacity.
More wine, good wife! A cup for Master Bruno.

BRUNO: You do me honour, sir.

BRUNO *seats himself, a little uncertainly under the disapproving*

gaze of the Prior. DONA DARIA *refills their glasses and offers a cup
to Bruno. She hesitates a moment, and then retires to her window
seat.* BRUNO *sniffs the wine.*

BRUNO: A better vintage
   Than the tavern-lees. Your health, good sirs!
      He drinks alone and then waits uncertainly.
MOCENIGO: Master Bruno, you have travelled much.
BRUNO: I am, sir, the most practised gallivant!
MOCENIGO: You have met high and low upon your journeys.
BRUNO (*flattered*): I have been lector to the King of France,
   I have disputed in Oxford, I am friend
   To learned lords in England – yet in truth,
   I have lived lowly, too – with poxy sailors
   And their trulls, horse-traders, pedlars,
   Wandering charlatans . . .
MOCENIGO: So, tell us, Bruno,
   – There is rebellion in the air and schism
   And heresy – What moves the common folk
   Here in Venice, there in Wittenberg?
      BRUNO, *still tipsy, but touched at a tender point, weighs the
   question, and then answers it with gradually increasing eloquence.*
BRUNO: What moves them? Beh! Hunger will make a riot.
   Yet, hand out bread and onions, it will die
   By sunrise.
   Lust? That's a disturber, too.
   I saw today a fellow cut from breast
   To belly-button for a tavern girl –
   But when you talk rebellion, heresy
   And deep disorders – ah! That's another tale!
TAVERNA (*sharp interest*): Tell it, Master Bruno. We who sit
   Upon the powder-keg would like to know
   What lights the fuse!
BRUNO (*eager*): Light! That's the word!
   The abracadabra spell that springs the door
   Into tomorrow. The light comes slowly, but –

By God! – it comes, to clown and chimney-sweep
And plodding serf.

PRIOR GABRIELLI: I do not understand.
Is this some new and specious revelation.

BRUNO: New to them. – But specious, no! Look!
On my master's book-shelves, there are maps
Which show the world is flat and that it ends
Just past the Pillars of Hercules, where flames
And horrid beasts devour lost sailor-men.
– There are no beasts! There are the golden lands
Cristoforo Colombo found, the Indies
And the seaways to Cathay! That's light!
Then there's Copernicus, and after him,
– Who knows? – An infinite universe of suns,
And moons and undiscovered earths!

PRIOR GABRIELLI (*snorts*): Seductive novelties!

BRUNO: But, Prior, they wake
Men's minds to questioning. Who drew the dragons
On the maps? Cartographers or quacks?
Who says the Pope sees all creation plain
An hour after they have elected him?
Who says a king rules by God-given right?
There is no king in Venice. Does God dispense
One right in Spain, another, different, here?
The people ask, Prior! Their questions make
The groundswell, and the tidal wave comes after.

PRIOR GABRIELLI: This is sedition!

DONA DARIA *gets up and moves towards the group.*

BRUNO: To ask a question? Come!
If God be God and man a creature made
In image of the divine intelligence,
His noblest function is the search for truth.

PRIOR GABRIELLI: The truth is on deposit in the world,
Set there by Christ, interpreted by those
Who are his lawful delegates. You, sir,

Talk sophistry! You . . .

    DONA DARIA *intervenes, gently, but firmly.*

DONA DARIA: Good Prior, our scholar
  Did but answer truthfully a question
  Set by my husband. We may disagree,
  But not insult his probity.

PRIOR GABRIELLI: Madam,
  I am reproved.

    BRUNO *gets up.*

BRUNO: I beg to be excused.

MOCENIGO: I recommend the broth. Good wife, attend
  Our scholar's needs!

    DONA DARIA *takes Bruno's arm and leads him out.* MOCENIGO
    throws back his head and laughs.

MOCENIGO: So there you have it, friends!
  The truth, spoken in wine!

TAVERNA: More than that!
  I am with the Prior. You harbour here
  Sedition and a rabble-rousing rogue
  To sell it in the streets!

MOCENIGO *(cold and dangerous)*: Should you not ask,
  As a discreet and careful emissary,
  Seeking friends, the wherefore and the why?

TAVERNA *(relaxes apologetically)*: I should. I do. I am saddle-sore
  And sleepless. I beg you, grant me absolution
  For bad manners.

PRIOR GABRIELLI *(placating)*: We have a common care,
  A common purpose.

MOCENIGO: A mutual trust, I hope?

TAVERNA: We have.

MOCENIGO: Good!

    He gets up, crosses to a bureau, unlocks it and brings out a sealed
    document. He returns holding it ostentatiously in his two hands.

MOCENIGO: This is our treaty, then.
  Rome is for Mocenigo. I for Rome,

On promise to restore, when I am come
To power in the Republic, all the rights
Of Mother Church, to root out heresy
And those who, on whatever pretext, teach
Or publish it.

TAVERNA: And the warranty?

MOCENIGO (*holds up document*): This! – A denunciation, notarized,
Over the name and seal of Mocenigo,
Of one Giordano Bruno, fugitive monk
    and heretic, whom for security,
Surveillance and recording of his crimes,
I have kept in my house.

He hands the document to the Prior and turns to Taverna.

MOCENIGO: You are witness,
For His Holiness. The document
Is now delivered to the Inquisitor.

The PRIOR accepts the document. He is puzzled and surprised.
There is a long silence. TAVERNA breaks it.

TAVERNA: Prior – with much respect – you have a case
In hand. Go, set the wheels a-turning, eh!

PRIOR GABRIELLI (*flustered*): Immediately! My Lords!
    The PRIOR exits.

TAVERNA: Mocenigo,
Noble to noble, tell me something!

MOCENIGO: What?

TAVERNA: Why would you, who have no need of rank,
Money, respect or credit, sell a man?

MOCENIGO: Why? We have had a council – Trent!
Its decrees – and mark me when I say it! –
Cut Europe like a cheese. Henceforth we are
Catholics and non-believers. How long
Can such a perilous division last?
A hundred years? Five hundred? I shall be dead
Before the outcome. So I place a bet
On the short run. Europe, at the core,

Is Christian. Ergo, the Church must win. This Bruno?
– A pawn! It is expedient for one
To die, to save a multitude. Objections?

TAVERNA: None. Just so we know the rules and play
The game accordingly. Let's dine!

MOCENIGO: And drink
A safer wine than Bruno's, eh?

They exit laughing. BORTOLO *enters, and resets the room. He
extinguishes all the candles except one candlabron which he sets on
the table. He gathers up the used glasses and goes out. A few
moments later* BRUNO *and* DONA DARIA *enter.* BRUNO *is sober
now and* DONA DARIA *is chiding him affectionately.*

DONA DARIA: Bruno!
Bruno! I have never known a man,
So lovable and so recalcitrant.
Why do you drink?

BRUNO: I am a toss-pot. Simple!

DONA DARIA: No! I find you sober, night after night
Worrying your texts; and then I see you,
Black devils on your back, beating your head
Bloody against invisible walls. Bruno,
I wish that I could hold you then, against
This breast of mine – which is not mine, but his
Who married me – and calm you into silence.
Your tongue will hang you yet.

BRUNO: I know.

DONA DARIA: They hate you.
And they harass you.

BRUNO: Harass me, yes!
But hate me? No, dear innocent, they need me!

DONA DARIA: Need you?

BRUNO: They do: Every sect and state
Needs enemies, else it will die of bloating
And prosperity. Our Mother Church,
Needs such a one as I, whom she can take

D

And say, 'Look, this is a heretic!
This is Antichrist!' Then – ah, – then! –
Little by little bend him – never break! –
But bend, with soft persuasion,
Argument and loneliness,
– That's the real racking, loneliness! –
To a confession of the Faith, free,
Willing, humble, full of sad remorse.
See what they have then! One to recant for all,
One stone to beat a million breasts
Into a penitent salvation. – My texts,
Where are they?

    DONA DARIA *goes to the bookshelves and picks out the tomes.*

DONA DARIA: Here!

    She lays the tomes on the table and opens them.

BRUNO (*wondering*): You know the pages!

DONA DARIA: The words!
  The very syllables . . . (*quotes*) 'De Immenso',
  'A poem by Filippo Bruno, called
  Giordano, Doctor of Philosophy,
  In which he treats of false astronomy,
  Of unity and of the infinite.' –
  Now, praise your pupil!

BRUNO (*grins*): In another time,
  Another body, a better estate than this,
  Richer and wiser, I should have married her!

DONA DARIA: Marriage, my little monk, is just a contract,
  Publicly endorsed. The afterward,
  The living of it, the loving in it, ah!
  That's the apple-core!

BRUNO: You are not loved?

DONA DARIA: No, and yet I love!

BRUNO (*lightly*): The remedy's
  A loving lover.

DONA DARIA: No! I cannot split
  My woman's self into a courtesan,
  A wife . . .
BRUNO: I would not wish it on you. I would . . .
DONA DARIA: What? . . .

    BRUNO *does not answer. He takes her hand and kisses it, without passion, but with great tenderness.*

BRUNO: Go to bed, my lady. Leave me
  To this sterility. But when you pray,
  Give me a moment's memory.

    He bends to his books. DONA DARIA *waits, reluctant to go.*

DONA DARIA: Bruno?
BRUNO: Yes?
DONA DARIA: Do you ever pray?
BRUNO: Sometimes.
DONA DARIA: How?
BRUNO: Go to bed.
DONA DARIA: Please pray with me.
BRUNO: Oh, God!
  Why do you torment me?
DONA DARIA: Pray with me!

    For a long and agonizing moment, BRUNO *battles with himself, then, tight and unhappy, he pushes himself out of his chair.*

BRUNO: Come to the window!

    They both cross to the window. BRUNO *parts the curtains and throws open the casement. Moonlight streams into the room.* BRUNO *gathers himself and strikes an attitude. He begins on a note of bitter irony and then slips unconsciously into a moving self-revelation.*

BRUNO: The prayer of Giordano Bruno,
  Penny philosopher and one-time priest,
  Magician by repute and heretic
  By imputation. fomentor of sedition,
  Boozer, braggart, fraud, and merry-Andrew
  Dancing his jig upon the mountain top,

Waiting for star-fire . . . O God, if God there be!
O Christ, if they did not kill you forever
On your Calvary! O mother of Christ,
Who saw what men could do to one who heard
An alien music! Bend to me, be tender.
I am blind and deaf and dumb. And yet,
I do see visions, shout a kind of praise,
Feel in my pulse apocalyptic drums.

They are so absorbed in the prayer, that they do not hear the measured approach of the guards.

BRUNO: The visions may be false. I do not know.
The praise may be a blasphemy. Forgive it.
The drums – O God, you set my heart a-pounding!
Whisper, just once, 'Be still. You are at home
And safe!'

At this moment, BORTOLO *enters and behind him an officer and four* SOLDIERS *of the civil guard.*

OFFICER: Giordano Bruno!

They turn, shocked.

BRUNO: I am he!

OFFICER: By order of the Council of the Ten,
At the request of the Inquisitors
of Holy Mother Church, you are arrested,
Ordered into custody!

BRUNO *is very calm.*

BRUNO: The charge?

OFFICER: None! Only the order of the Ten.

BRUNO: I have been denounced?

OFFICER: I do not know.

DONA DARIA (*bursts out*): Captain, you are guilty of a trespass.
This is my husband's house!

BRUNO (*grim*): Madam, I fear
Your husband's hand directs the puppet-show!

DONA DARIA (*horror*): No!

BRUNO: Bortolo, fetch my cloak!

    BORTOLO *hesitates and then goes reluctantly.*

BRUNO (*very gently*): And you,

  Dear lady, please – please go to bed!

    She cannot make the move. She breaks and clings to him. He stands very erect, holding her and facing his captors.

CURTAIN

ACT TWO

SCENE ONE

Venice, 1592. *The prison of the Doge's Palace.*

The set is a composite, on two levels. The lower level is Bruno's cell, a dismal hole furnished with a pallet bed. (As an annex to the cell, there is an inset which, when lit, shows a torture-roon and a torturer.)

The upper level is the examination room, where Bruno confronts the tribunal of the Inquisition.

When the scene opens, BRUNO, *dressed now in a shabby, monkish costume with a cowl, is being led by a guard from his cell to the examination room. The Inquisitors await him, seated at their table, with their books and documents ranged before them:*

The Inquisitors are: PRIOR GABRIELLI, *Presiding;* LUDOVICO TAVERNA, *the Papal Nuncio on his right;* LAURENTIO PRIOLI, *the Patriarch of Venice, on his left. At one end of the table, a little apart, sits* TOMMASO MOROSINI, *Assessor of the Republic of Venice. At the other end is the* RECORDER.

Bruno's GUARD *stands him before the tribunal. There is a long silence, broken by the Prior.*

PRIOR GABRIELLI (*formal*): Filippo Giordano Bruno, sometimes called
The Nolan, Doctor of Philosophy,
Presbyter, Clerk regular of the order
Of Friars Preachers, you are summoned here
To answer or refute, sundry and various
Denunciations, touching your published works,
Your lectures, your opinions, whether expressed

In private or in public.
    BRUNO *throws back his cowl and holds himself erect and strong.*
BRUNO: Most Reverend,
  Of what am I convicted?
PRIOR GABRIELLI (*shocked*): Convicted, sir?
  Of nothing. Here we are concerned with truth.
  We make an inquisition into charges
  Laid against you.
BRUNO: By whom?
PRIOR GABRIELLI: You may not know.
BRUNO: Their credit, Prior, and credibility,
  Touch me most intimately – threaten my life.
  How do I challenge men who have no name,
  No face?
PRIOR GABRIELLI: *We* test them, sir, as we do you.
BRUNO (*sharp*): But I am here, my lords, a prisoner
  While they go free. You prove them perjured liars,
  I am still robbed of these my precious days
  Of light and liberty. Is this a justice?
PRIOR GABRIELLI: It is the method of the law.
BRUNO: And I
  Have no redress against this loaded law?
PRIOR GABRIELLI: None, sir. We are the servants of what exists,
  Until a later wisdom changes it.
  The Clerk will read the charges.
BRUNO: A moment, please.
PRIOR GABRIELLI (*testy*): Yes? What now?
BRUNO: My cell is damp. My food
  A bite above starvation. I am racked
  With a rheumatic swelling in every joint.
  I beg the courtesy of a chair.
    The PRIOR *snaps his fingers at the* GUARD, *who brings a chair
  for* BRUNO. *He seats himself.*
PRIOR GABRIELLI (*to Clerk*): The charges.
    The RECORDER *picks up a document and begins to read.*

RECORDER (*reads formally*): The first denunciation charges thus:
  'This Bruno said: the Eucharistic rite,
  – Bread changed to flesh and blood – is blasphemy!
  The Mass is magic for the ignorant.
  The Trinity – Three Persons in one God –
  Is an impossibility. A virgin
  Giving birth without a man to seed her
  Is a fraud. The miracles of Christ
  Were conjuring tricks. Men's souls migrate
  To animals. The universe endures,
  Eternal, infinite – a million suns,
  Uncounted earths. The Scholar further said
  All priests and friars are asses, selling straw
  To other asses. The first Apostles taught
  By preaching and good works; but now the Church
  Converts by force and not by love. Man must
  Use his own liberty to come to God.
  Our Church corrupts itself and makes of God
  An image of its own corruption.' Then,
  Concerning marriage and the marriage act,
  The Nolan thus proclaimed: 'The Church doth sin
  In making sins of what serves man so well
  And pleasantly' –
    There is a slight pause. The Inquisitors study Bruno.
BRUNO (*relaxes and laughs*): That's quite a catalogue!
TAVERNA: Of vicious errors!
BRUNO: Too many for one man!
MOROSINI (*an ironic languor*): And written in anger, too. It
  tastes of gall,
  Splenetic indigestion.
BRUNO: Thank you, my lord.
  And may I add a gloss? This document,
  Contains a contradiction. First it says
  I am a kind of atheist, who rejects
  The sum and substance of the Faith. Then –

God help us, gentlemen! – in the same breath,
I plead an apostolic love, a need
To come to God in Christian liberty,
Reform within the assembly of the Faith.
What does he want, my nameless enemy?
To flip a ducat for a bet and have it
Fall head and tail at once?

PRIOLI: Then you deny
Every and all the statements in the charge?

BRUNO: No, Excellency. I deny the import
And conclusion of the whole. I claim
A malice and malversation of my words.
Look! You are three clerics, schoolmen, trained
In argument and disputation. So
You know how you were taught – by pro and contra.
One day you stand in the debate and say
'There is no God! – refute me!' Another day
You take another stand. It is the method,
Honourable and approved, from Plato
To Aquinas. When you use it, Prior,
Are you a heretic? No more am I!
But any fool or knave, hearing you talk,
Could wrench it out of frame and burn you for it!

PRIOR GABRIELLI (*to Recorder*): You will note that the accused
    does not
Deny the formal words ascribed to him.
He does deny the taint of heresy.
He claims a malice in the informant.

MOROSINI: Note
As well the evident discrepancy
And contradiction in the document.

RECORDER: It is done.

MOROSINI (*more cold*): Request on my behalf,
As spokesman for the Serenissima,
A new interrogation of the writer.

TAVERNA: I approve that.

PRIOLI: And I.

PRIOR GABRIELLI: It shall be done.
(*To Bruno.*) Now, master Bruno, with some justice you
Object anonymous testimony. We
Grant the objection. Will you grant to us
The right to stand, upon two other grounds,
– The public record of your life, the books,
Which bear your name upon the title-page?

BRUNO: I grant it yes, but on conditions.

TAVERNA: What!

BRUNO: That I may still interpret and explain
My own words and myself.

PRIOLI: Should they need
Interpretation?

BRUNO (*stoutly*): Always, Eminence!
You lift your skirts on the traghetto, you
Expose – saving your Grace – a pubic part.
A modest maid cries gross indecency!
You claim a simple need – to piss or burst.
The act still needs explaining!

PRIOLI (*laughs*): Granted!

BRUNO: Thank you.

*The PRIOR takes time to consult his papers. Then, a very
formidable lawyer, he begins his brief.*

PRIOR GABRIELLI: We begin then with the man – Filippo
Bruno, born in fifteen forty eight
At Nola, in Campania. Studied in Naples,
Logic, humanities and dialectic.

BRUNO (*succumbs to garrulity*): Good teachers, too – the best! –
Teofilo
Vairano, Vincenzo Colle il Sarnese.
I remember them with love.

PRIOR: At seventeen,
You became a novice in the convent

Of Saint Dominic. The record states
'An avid student, prodigious memory,
A captious tongue, a will not easily bent
To discipline.'

BRUNO (*grins*): Hold our youth against us
Prior, we should all be gallows meat!

> *This brings a laugh from all except the* PRIOR. *He goes on relentlessly checking off the notes.*

PRIOR GABRIELLI: You took vows then – promised solemnly
To live in poverty, in chastity,
Obedient subjection to the Rule
Of our most holy Founder, yes?

BRUNO: I did.

PRIOR GABRIELLI: You were ordained a priest?

BRUNO: I was.

PRIOR GABRIELLI (*rams the point home*): And then you broke the
vows. You fled the convent
And the priesthood. Yes or no?

BRUNO: Yes.

> *The Prior has scored his first point. He lets the tribunal digest it for a moment.*

MOROSINI (*a probing irony*): Why did you do it, Master Bruno?

BRUNO: Why?
That is old history, my lord. I'll try
To reconstruct it. You have never been
A monk?

MOROSINI: Never, thank God!

BRUNO: A monastery,
My lord, is like a very little world,
Shut in behind stone walls. There are few saints,
Some who live in simple rectitude,
And others who, within the Church or out,
Would sell their sisters for a pastry-cake.
In this little world, there are no women,
Only men, who in despite of fasts

And penances and prayerful nights,
Grow rank with their own seed, and then, like bulls
Penned in a common pasture, vent their rage
On one another. I was first accused
Of an impiety. I would not wear
Medallions of the saints around my neck,
Clustered like Bacchus' grapes. I still preferred
The simple image of the Crucified. Another time,
I found a brother monk fumbling my papers,
Sniffing for heresy, like a pig for truffles!
I hid them from him – in a privy! Boh!
Guilt was presumed and I arraigned for trial,
By Master-General in Rome. I had
No answer to conspiracy. I fled!

TAVERNA: 'The guilty fleeth when no man pursueth.'
  That's in the scripture!

BRUNO (*anger*): Do not judge me, sir,
  By tags and texts! True justice is dispensed
  Far otherwise!

TAVERNA: You are insolent, sir.

BRUNO (*savage*): Sit here and feel the sword-blade on your neck!
  Let me pelt you with scraps of Holy Writ.
  See how you like it!

PRIOLI: We must control ourselves!
  We are a court, and not a bear pit! Bruno,
  This flight of yours does bear a colour of guilt.

BRUNO: I know it, Eminence.

PRIOLI: Had you then the wit
  To face down your accusers and to trust
  The loving-kindness of our Mother Church,
  You might not now stand in such jeopardy.

BRUNO: Eminence, at twenty-five, a rebel
  And afraid, our Mother Church was like
  A giantess, neglectful of her brood,
  Careless of all their miseries!

PRIOLI: She was
  And is your mother.
BRUNO: I, her son, still find
  Her breasts are dry, her hands are less than gentle.
  May I stretch my aching joints?
PRIOLI: Be free!

  BRUNO *gets up awkwardly, flexing his cramped muscles.*
  PRIOLI *watches him with pity and adds a gentle word.*
PRIOLI: We are not gaolers, but inquisitors,
  Seeking a common truth.
TAVERNA (*springs a trap*): And, Brother Bruno,
  This would be one truth! You went to Zurich
  And became a Calvinist!

  BRUNO *is at bay again. This is his real enemy.*
BRUNO: I did!
TAVERNA: A renegade! A chaser after false
  And alien creeds!
BRUNO: No, sir! A puzzled soul
  Trying now that, now this, to find a hat
  That fits his bursting brainbox!
MOROSINI: And you found it?
BRUNO (*a tired grin*): No! This tetchy imp who rides my back
  Forbade me such a peace. I quarrelled, sir,
  With those Swiss sobersides and spent a time
    in Gaol!
TAVERNA (*heavy irony*): So! It seems, good brother Bruno,
  You are neither fish nor fowl. Among
  The heretics you are the orthodox,
  And with the faithful, more an atheist
  Than Julian the Apostate.
BRUNO (*quietly*): Excellency,
  Have you ever had a son?
TAVERNA: Never!
BRUNO: Nor I. But, if we had, would we not see
  Him grope and strain from infancy to boyhood,

Boy to man, testing himself against
A strange, strange world? Would we not pity him
And stretch a father's hand to lift him up
From darkness into light?

TAVERNA: But, if and when
He comes to manhood, must we hold him safe
From all his follies?

BRUNO: If we love, we try.
(*A shrewd challenge.*)
The Church is our common Mother, so I ask,
How do you see, sirs? A son, a brother,
– or an enemy?

TAVERNA: We do not know.
A heretic can have no part in Christ.
Or the Assembly of His Holy Ones.
(*He picks references out of his papers.*)
We note, you see, in all your wanderings,
This curious circumstance – Your patrons and
Your friends – in England, Germany and France,
Are all the rebel breed of Protestants.
Your lectures and your disputations, such
As were delated to us, all reject
The classic lines of Christian argument. (*Sarcasm.*)
You must not blame us if we smell at least
A wolf under the sheepskin!

PRIOLI (*hastily*): In spite of that,
We wish to treat with you in charity.

BRUNO: All of you? You, Prior, Excellency, You?

MOROSINI (*cool advice*): Brother Bruno. Do not bet your life
Upon our Christianity. Convince us!

BRUNO (*helpless shrug*): How?

PRIOR GABRIELLI: Be seated, sir.
BRUNO *wilts a little and seats himself.*
Your books are you.
No argument?

BRUNO: No argument. Except —

TAVERNA (*contempt*): Always exceptions! Never an answer plain.

MOROSINI (*ironic defence*): The man is a philosopher! He needs
A definition of the terms!

TAVERNA (*shrugs*): So be it!

BRUNO (*a curious, pleading note*): Prior, like me, you are Dominican?

PRIOR GABRIELLI: Yes.

BRUNO: We learned the same theology.

PRIOR GABRIELLI: Yes.

BRUNO: Our masters said free speculation
Is allowed, on every matter but
The substance of the Faith. Do you agree?

PRIOR GABRIELLI: I do.

BRUNO: So, when I reason in my books
Of nature and the natural order – right
Or wrong – I am beyond attainder. Yes?

PRIOR GABRIELLI (*dubious*): Yes. But if you make one step
beyond
The natural into the realm of faith,
You fall under the law.

BRUNO: Whose law, Prior?
Before I piously consent to hang
Myself with this your codex, may we please
Examine and interpret it together?

TAVERNA (*furious*): My God! The man's a legal trickster.
Spinning a web of court-room sophistries,
Just to distract us!

BRUNO: Am I, Sir Nuncio?
(*He speaks now, with a great and grave dignity.*)
Let me show you what I am. One man
Without an advocate or single friend
In court. I have not slept too well because
Of damp and rats inside my cell.
I have not prepared my case. You –

Only you have seen the documents.
Besides, there is no candle in my cell
To read by. I face you – four judges and
A clerk! Behind you, what? The majesty
Of Venice and her Empire, the might of Rome,
And all the Princes who support her, all
The army of the orthodox. Give me
At least, the time to argue for my life.
– Or finish this base comedy, and burn me
Now!

He has silenced them for the moment. Out of the silence, a new
man begins to emerge, slowly, from the PRIOR. *He is not and will*
never be a hero. But he begins to walk a certain way up the mountain.

PRIOR GABRIELLI: Your point is taken, Brother. I
Do urge upon my colleagues to refrain
From harassing the accused and to respect
His right of argument. (*To Bruno.*) Bruno, you asked
A statement of the law. We put it thus.
Our Saviour, Jesus Christ, came down to earth,
God in human flesh and gave us all,
A revelation of eternal truth.
He left, to Peter and his successors,
The keys of Heaven, authority to preach,
Interpret and unfold the moral code
Implicit in the truth. That is the Right
Of Peter; the rest of us, Bishops and Priests,
May use the right, by lawful delegation
Only. Are you answered, Brother?

BRUNO: No!
I have to ask, because my liberty
Depends on it, who says with certainty
What is a matter of faith, and what of proper
Speculation?

PRIOR GABRIELLI: The limits are defined
From time to time by Papal documents,

The councils and the Church's common mind.

BRUNO: But the limits change. So what may burn
Me now, tomorrow may make me a Saint and Doctor
Of the Church. You see my problem! Christ
Had never heard of Transubstantiation.
I vote for Christ, I am baptized into
The Christian family. – Am I then cast out
For a new word Saint Paul might choke on!

TAVERNA: Do you reject the word?

BRUNO: I have not said so.

PRIOR GABRIELLI (*shrugs*): We can argue this into absurdity.
You asked a statement of the law. You have it.
Begin now with these books: 'Of Infinite Worlds'.
And, 'Of the Principal and Primal Cause'.

He holds up the volumes, displaying the title pages. He makes a
lawyer's switch.

A curious thing! The title-pages say
'Printed in Venice'. Were they not, in fact,
Issued in England?

BRUNO (*humbled*): Yes.

TAVERNA: Another lie!
A little one, but most significant.

BRUNO (*lamely*): My publishers advised it.

TAVERNA: You connived!

BRUNO: For better money. Yes!

TAVERNA: Does this not
Make you a venal man?

BRUNO: It does, perhaps,
But I was very poor.

It is another mark against him. The tribunal notes it silently.

PRIOR GABRIELLI: In these works
You state, the Universe extends beyond
Our vision, to infinity. Our world is
One of many.

BRUNO: Yes.

E

PRIOR GABRIELLI: Are we not
  At one stride into heresy? Is not
  Infinity an attribute of God,
  And only God?
BRUNO (*eager*): I say that God himself
  Is co-extensive with his universe!
PRIOR GABRIELLI (*riffles pages*): You say more! 'What we call
    the Creator
  Is that which animates us all'. Already
  You are out of nature into faith.
  You are in conflict —
BRUNO: I – I did not mean it
  Thus.
TAVERNA: But thus you wrote it. Your books, you said,
  Are you!
        BRUNO *is silenced. The* PRIOR *presses his advantage. He gets up
    and, carrying one of the volumes, goes to Bruno.*
PRIOR GABRIELLI: Now read the passage I have marked.
        BRUNO *takes the book and reads hesitantly.*
BRUNO: 'The soul, the anima, being a thrust
  Of the Eternal Energy, continues
  After one body's death, to animate
  Another envelope, human or animal.'
PRIOR GABRIELLI: Stop there!
        *He takes back the book and returns to his place at the table. He is
    very grave and very clear, as befits a good advocate.*
  Brother Bruno, here we have
  Two propositions. Both are yours, and both
  On face of it – heretical. The Church
  Has always taught that human souls do not
  Migrate. That God, eternal, infinite,
  Is infinitely greater than his own
  Creation. Sustains it, but is separate!
PRIOLI (*frowning*): I am concerned. The statements correspond
  With the first charges read.

TAVERNA (*sour triumph*): I think we'll find
  As we walk Brother Bruno down the road,
  That the denunciation he objected
  Is a true bill of particulars,
  Written by an honest man – as shocked as we
  By the opinions of this self-styled scholar.
  What say you, Brother? – Better confess it now,
  Than stretch the patience and credulity
  Of this tribunal!
    Bruno's reply is less certain than his others. He is shaken and tries
  to play for time.
BRUNO: I will not confess.
  I stand on my first claim – freedom to enquire,
  Hold and express opinions on any subject
  In the natural order. I further claim
  Everything that I have written or said,
  Conforms in substance to the Deposit of Faith.
  Give me paper, pens and ink, give me
  My books, a copy of the bill against me,
  Time – and some light within my cell – I'll prove
  My orthodoxy, point by point. Errors
  There may be, but of expression, not intent.
  These I will happily recant and edit out
  Of future printings.
TAVERNA (*laughs contemptuously*): There's a Serpentine
  Concession! 'I am absolutely right,
  But if I am wrong, I'll change it overnight!'
  This fellow will keep us here a twelvemonth
  With his sleight of hand. Give him paper
  Enough, he'll scribble us all into the grave!
MOROSINI (*cool as ever*): He has a right to answer, does he
    not?
  He has a duty to recant when once
  Convinced of error. He offers that. Why not
  Accept?

TAVERNA: Because I do not trust him! He shifts
　And changes like a weather cock! He is
　A liar, self-confessed!

PRIOLI: In spite of that
　We have a clear commission: sober study,
　A dispassionate verdict, a sentence fit
　For what misdeeds are proved, a merciful
　Concern for the immortal soul of this
　Our troubled brother.

TAVERNA: I say we execute
　Our charge the better, if we cut away
　Confusion!

PRIOLI: How?

TAVERNA (cold): Put Bruno to the Question!
　　　The demand shocks them all. BRUNO *sits in mute horror. The*
　　　PRIOR *grows a little larger.*

PRIOR GABRIELLI: No! I will not consent!

TAVERNA: You will! You must.

PRIOR GABRIELLI: The intention of the law is clear. The
　court
　Shall not put any man to torture who
　Has not displayed obduracy and contempt.

PRIOLI: That is true.

TAVERNA: I say Giordano Bruno
　Is a hardened contumacious cheat.

MOROSINI: I disagree. He stands in peril here,
　He may use any tactic in defence.

TAVERNA: The Court being disagreed, then I invoke
　Authority. Eminence, you are
　The Patriarch of Venice.

PRIOLI: Yes.

TAVERNA: From whom
　Did you receive your bishopric, your title?

PRIOLI: From the Pope. The Vicar of Christ.

TAVERNA: Prior,

Who gives the Preaching Friars their brief, their high
Responsibility within the Church?

PRIOR GABRIELLI: Rome. His Holiness.

TAVERNA: This tribunal
Sits by his order?

PRIOLI: Yes, it does.

TAVERNA: And I,
As Papal Nuncio, here represent
That same high person Clement, by God's Grace,
Head of the Universal Church. With this
My patent, in the name of God, I say,
Giordano Bruno shall immediately
Be put to the Question.

BRUNO *breaks and cries out.*

BRUNO: You cannot do this!

TAVERNA: Be silent! Gentlemen, what say you all?

MOROSINI: A small reminder, Excellency!

TAVERNA: Yes?

MOROSINI: The instruments of death and torture are
At the disposal of the secular arm
And not the Church. Not here, in Venice, sir!

TAVERNA: You refuse me, then?

MOROSINI (*smooth*): Not yet. I wait upon
A formal and polite request from Rome
– Through you – to the Republic, which in this court,
Is me!

TAVERNA, *hating him, is forced to accept the diplomacy. He
recovers himself and makes a very formal request.*

TAVERNA: Messer Morosini! I request
Formally and with profound respect,
Co-operation to complete the work
Of this most Holy Roman Inquisition!

MOROSINI (*studious deliberation*): To aid the Faith, and, further,
to cement
The friendship of Rome and Venice – I consent.

PRIOR GABRIELLI: I register objection!

TAVERNA (*contempt*): Note it, Clerk!

> BRUNO *is on his feet, trembling.*

BRUNO: You are horrible men! You have no pity!
   You play a power game with human lives,
   You crucify the Christ you say you love,
   In us his helpless children.

TAVERNA: Take him, guards!

> *The* GUARDS *take* BRUNO *out roughly. Instinctively the* IN-
> QUISITORS *stand. The lights dim slowly in the examination room*
> *and come up bright in the lower cell, where a* MASKED TORTURER
> *waits amid his sinister array of instruments.* BRUNO *is led to the rack*
> *and as the* GUARDS *begin to strip him.*

BLACK OUT

The same. Night. Two lanterns hung on the wall throw a dim light on the examination room. A sleepy GUARD *sits on a stool at the door of Bruno's cell. The cell is in darkness. Two figures, cloaked and hooded, enter the examination room. They are not immediately identifiable in the dim light, but one is* MOROSINI *and the other* DONA DARIA.

The GUARD *wakes up and stands to attention.* MOROSINI *leads Dona Daria to the table and seats her there. He approaches the guard. He indicates the door of the cell, but does not speak. The* GUARD *unlocks it. He takes a lantern from the wall and leads* MOROSINI *into the cell.*

Now the examination room is very dim and the cell is illuminated.

BRUNO, *wrapped in his cloak and covered by an old blanket, lies huddled on the pallet bed.*

MOROSINI *and the* GUARD *stand looking down at him.* MOROSINI *waves the guard away. The* GUARD *sets down the lantern and exits, closing the door, but not locking it.* MOROSINI *pulls a wooden stool to the side of the bed and sits. He throws back his hood, revealing himself. He is still the ironic assessor.*

MOROSINI (*to the sleeping man*): Poor little man!
　　So puffed up with your fine philosophies,
　　You cannot even read the weather signs!
　　The thunder's rolling round your ears, and you –
　　You are still listening for nightingales! (*He shakes Bruno.*)
　　Wake up! Wake up, Master Bruno!

　　BRUNO *stirs, groaning into wakefulness. He has been racked. Every move is a torment. His speech is spasmodic and painful.*

BRUNO: No!

  No more, I beg you! Who – who are you?

MOROSINI: A friend!

    He holds the lantern up to his face. BRUNO *recognizes him and lies back wearily.*

BRUNO: Such friends! God save me from my foes!

MOROSINI: He cannot, being a prisoner like you

  Of theologians and inquisitors!

  I can, and will.

BRUNO: You! I remember now!

  You sold me to the torturers – to aid

  The Faith . . .

MOROSINI (*amiably*): Not sold! Just lent! To teach you, friend,

  A necessary wisdom!

BRUNO: Give me water,

  I am burning up!

    There is a wooden pail and a ladle at hand. MOROSINI *scoops up water and offers it.* BRUNO *cannot help himself.* MOROSINI *hoists him and holds the ladle to his lips. He drinks, chattery and greedy, slopping the liquid. He lies back exhausted.*

MOROSINI: Can you hear me?

BRUNO: Yes.

MOROSINI: And understand?

BRUNO (*a relic of humour*): I understand, my lord,

  Only the believing's difficult!

MOROSINI (*genuine admiration*): I like you, Bruno. You are much a man!

  But not enough – no man is ever enough

  To beat the last turn of the rack, the last

  Hot iron on the foot-soles.

BRUNO: Go away!

MOROSINI: Do you know who betrayed you?

BRUNO: Mocenigo.

MOROSINI: More, my friend! Ciotto the bookseller,

Brother Celestine, the Capuchin,
Graziano the Neopolitan,
Those two were prison friends with whom you joked,
Shared bread and cocked a snook at piety.
– All of them told their little tales upstairs.
Volumes of petty treachery, enough
To burn a dozen Brunos!

BRUNO: I am sick
Of this sick world!

MOROSINI: They will not let you out
So easily. They will tread you, Brother,
Like a grape, down to the pips and skin!
And the skin they'll nail up on the door
And say, 'Look, this was an heresiarch!
Another Arius, another Lather?'

BRUNO: Heresiarch! My God, how do they dream
These calumnies!

MOROSINI: They do not dream. They are
The most pragmatical of men. As I am.

BRUNO: What do you want?

MOROSINI: To cheat the Mocenigo,
Spit in his shifty eye. Do you know yet,
My baby Socrates, why you were sold?

BRUNO: He wanted me to teach him magic. I
Could not. He thought I cheated him.

MOROSINI: O God! The innocence of scholars! Look!
You were a gift from heaven to Mocenigo!
He wants the favour of Rome. He thinks to buy it
With you, a bright new heretic!

BRUNO: But you?

MOROSINI: I want you to confess, tomorrow. Sign
Whatever abjuration they dictate.

BRUNO: And then?

MOROSINI: Then you belong to Venice, not
To Rome. We sentence you. A modest term

Of penance, in a pleasant convent, where
The wine is good and books are plentiful.
When you're forgotten, in a year or two,
We'll give you gold, safe conduct and a horse,
And send you packing in to Germany!

BRUNO (*bitter*): I wish I could believe the half of it!

MOROSINI: Unless I can convince you, you are lost!

BRUNO: Give me a grain of hope!

MOROSINI: Better than that.

He gets up, goes to the door of the cell, opens it, enters the examination room and beckons to DONA DARIA. *She crosses to him, still hooded and unrecognisable. She precedes him into the cell.*

She stands a moment looking down at Bruno. In a single movement, she kneels and throws back her hood. She is shaken by the sight of his extremity.

DONA DARIA: Master Bruno!

BRUNO: My lady!

He struggles to sit up, is cramped by a sudden pain and falls back gasping. DONA DARIA *turns to ask for help from* MOROSINI, *but he is already at the foot of the steps and closing the door. He crosses the examination room and takes the position she has left.*

DONA DARIA *throws off her cloak, opens her reticule and takes out a handkerchief, a vial of perfume and a small silver flask. She sprinkles perfume on the handkerchief and bathes his face with it.*

DONA DARIA (*anger*): Thank God I have
No children, lest I mother men like these!

BRUNO *raises a clawed hand to stroke her forehead. He is broken by weariness and relief.*

BRUNO: You are the first light I have seen. My own
Small star . . . !

DONA DARIA *takes his hand and studies it, horrorstruck.*

DONA DARIA: What have they done to you?

BRUNO (*small grin*): My lady,

They have a whole compendium of arts
To make us suffer.
   DONA DARIA *kisses the twisted hand, then holds it to her breast.*
DONA DARIA: My husband laid the charges?
BRUNO: He and the others. There is so much hate –
DONA DARIA: I have my share of it to spend!
BRUNO: Hush! Hush!
   (*He groans as a sudden pain takes him.*)
Forgive me! I am torn with cramps and rigors!
   DONA DARIA *reaches for the flask and holds it to his lips.*
DONA DARIA: Drink this! I had it from my apothecary,
  A liquor and an opiate to ease
  The pain.
   He drinks and she settles him back.
BRUNO: How came you here?
DONA DARIA (*bitter*): I used to be,
  – Before I knew the terror of the Church –
  A visitant of lazarets and prisons,
  – Our Lady of the Sorrows, that's the name
  We gave our little confraternity.
  I saw our noble Patriarch. I begged
  To visit you. He, piously, demurred,
  Then handed me to Morosini, who,
  Having no claim to piety, consented.
  So, I am here.
BRUNO: Morosini wants
  My recantation.
DONA DARIA (*eager*): So do I:
BRUNO (*utter bewilderment*): Of all
  The women in the world, not you!
DONA DARIA (*very gentle*): My love,
  – Yes, I can say it now, here, where there is
  No love! – My love, my master in magic arts,
  I have read all your books, dreamt all your dreams.
  I tell you, not one of them is worth your life.

BRUNO: How can you say that?

DONA DARIA (*deep loving pity*): You are so much a monk.
My dear, dear friend, so much a cloud-walker,
You do not see the violets in the grass.
Give me your hands. I kiss them. Hands that wrote
Visions that have transported me. But Bruno, (*she presses his
hands to her body*)
Let me feel here one stirring of new life,
One flush of milk into these breasts – and I
Renounce your visions for reality.
A life! A human life! Flesh and blood,
And that strange other thing, a human mind!
You are alive, my love. So let them burn
Every last book! You can write again!
Dead, they will scatter your ashes to the wind,
And who will hear the piping of your ghost
At midnight? Not even I.

BRUNO: I am so tired.

DONA DARIA: Good! The opiate is working.

BRUNO: Why – (*A great effort.*)
Why have you robbed me of my anger?

DONA DARIA: To give
You back your life.

BRUNO (*fighting darkness*): It is not enough!
A man, to live a man, has to know when
To die. (*A last effort.*) There must be reasons – reasons – !
He collapses. DONA DARIA *soothes him like a child.*

DONA DARIA: Sleep now!
My tired lover, who has never loved,
My stargazer whose constellations stand
Always in contradiction. Sleep . . . ! Sleep!
    BRUNO *sleeps. She draws the blanket tenderly about him, puts on
the cloak and hood, picks up the lantern and mounts to the examination room, as the guard locks the door. She crosses to* MOROSINI
who rises at her approach.

MOROSINI: Well my lady? Will he bend to what
　We plan for him?
DONA DARIA: I hope, I pray he will. (*A sudden cold threat.*)
　I pray, sir, if he does, that you will keep
　Your bargain!
MOROSINI (*sincere*): I will try.
DONA DARIA: No sir! Not try!
　Perform! (*A terrible simplicity.*) I promise you, if you do not,
　I will run mad in Venice, telling this tale,
　Shouting your plots on the Rialto, crying
　Your treachery in taverns.
　　　In a sudden, cold anger, MOROSINI *takes hold of her.*
MOROSINI: Understand me!
　Madam understand! Breathe but a word
　Of these our strategies, I'll have you dead
　Within a week, or bricked up in a cell
　Beside a church!
DONA DARIA: Do not threaten me!
MOROSINI (*relaxes a little*): I make no threat. I tell you simple
　　truth.
　We are all beleagured here. Rome,
　Is vowed to stamp out heresy, or else
　Europe is split forever. Venice is pledged
　To be the Most Serene Republic till
　The dawn of doomsday.
　Your noble husband wants
　The Doge's hat. – You want your scholar safe.
　Our councillors, myself. We want him free
　To thwart this scheming Nuncio of ours
　And put the evil eye on Mocenigo!
　Where do we end? We play with tarot cards,
　Who gets the hanging man? We do not know.
　We pity him and let him die, because
　We are all forest beasts who want to live!
　Well, madam?

DONA DARIA: Take me home!
MOROSINI (*ironic courtesy*): Your servant,
  Lady Mocenigo.
    They exit.

BLACK OUT

The same. Morning. The tribunal is assembled. The GUARDS *are posted.* MOCENIGO *sits in the chair, under re-examination.*

MOCENIGO (*testy*): I am troubled!
  Three times I have presented to this court,
  My written depositions. Why am I now
  Badgered with all these questions?
TAVERNA (*smooth*): Please, my lord,
  Permit an explanation. We do not,
  In Roman legal usage, imitate
  The Germans who, with plea and counterplea,
  Make a dispute for justice, like a joust
  Or tournament. We enquire, we delve,
  Like miners chipping at the dross
  To find the single vein of gold – the truth.
MOCENIGO (*cold*): Does your Excellency suggest that I,
  Over my hand and seal, compound untruth?
MOCENIGO: Not his Excellency, but the accused.
  He claimed – the record will confirm it –
  'Malice and malversation'.
MOCENIGO: He lies!
MOROSINI (*smooth*): Of course,
  But we must prove he lies.
TAVERNA (*a tart reminder*): Because he stands
  At risk – not you, my Lord, who have discharged
  A christian duty, and whom we hold safe.
MOCENIGO (*grudgingly mollified*): Now that I understand . . .

PRIOR GABRIELLI: We ask you this:
   The character of Bruno, how would you
   Describe it?
MOCENIGO (*studious moderation*): Well, at first sight, agreeable!
   Garrulous perhaps, but still a wit!
   Quick-tempered, passionate in argument.
   Sometimes, in his cups, he'll play buffoon,
   But sober, he can be learned and profound.
MOROSINI: Not stupid?
MOCENIGO: Never! On the contrary,
   Most devious and subtle.
MOROSINI: In the end,
   You did not like him?
MOCENIGO: I mistrusted him.
MOROSINI: He knew that?
MOCENIGO: Yes. I am jack-blunt, I make
   No secrets.
MOROSINI: Thank you. Please continue, Prior.
   The PRIOR *refers to his documents, then addresses Mocenigo.*
PRIOR GABRIELLI: Consider this part of your testimony:
   'One day, while walking out with Bruno – I
   Remember we were going to St. George
   The Greater for a Mass – he said these things:
   "Christ was a sad fellow, who seduced
   The people with his magus tricks. His friends
   Were better men than he, because they died
   Most willingly, while he feared death and tried
   To flee it!" '
MOCENIGO: I remember that.
TAVERNA: It was
   Plain heresy!
MOCENIGO: No less!
MOROSINI (*moves in for kill*): And yet the man,
   Who spoke it – subtle, devious,
   Knowing your rancour and mistrust – would put

A sword into your hands to kill him with.
Come, my friend!

MOCENIGO: I am insulted, sirs!

PRIOLI (*mildly*): Why so? Our learned colleague simply points
To certain contradictions, asking you
To make a true equation of the facts.

MOROSINI: Put it another way: which Bruno have we
In the cells? Yours? Or another man,
Quite different?

MOCENIGO (*battling for composure*): I do not understand
The import of the question.

MOROSINI: Slowly then,
We'll come to it. You know the little lane,
A minute from San Marco? The street of Dolls –
The vulgar have another name for it! –
Where they make children's puppets and marionettes?
Well, they begin with wooden manikins,
No face, no eyes, just limbs and trunk and head,
Each one alike. Then they begin to paint.
Six strokes and there's a Harlequin! Presto!
Mouth up! and there's a cheerful cavalier!
Mouth down! and there's a sad old Pantaloon!
Your Bruno, sir – and we know ours right well,
We stood and watched him racked. We heard him
    scream –
Is but a painted man. You see our problem? –
You paint too perfectly – no living man
Can match your jumping doll, be he a saint
Or satanist!

   MOCENIGO, *trapped, looks round the faces of the court. They are
all closed against him. He makes a desperate counter-attack.*

MOCENIGO: You have conspired to bring
Me to this moment.

PRIOLI (*his first real strength*): No, sir! We have not
Conspired!

MOCENIGO: I was hasty, Eminence.
Forgive me!

PRIOLI: You are forgiven. You may go.

MOCENIGO: But Eminence, my credit here? My name?
My reputation for integrity?

PRIOLI: Will have the weight which they deserve, when we
Deliver judgement! Sir, you are excused.

MOCENIGO takes one last look at the unfriendly faces and exits.
MOROSINI caps the exit with a sniper's shot at Taverna.

MOROSINI: There goes a man who thought to be a Doge!
If ever he wore the cap – God help us all.

PRIOR GABRIELLI (*to Guard*): Bring in the prisoner!

*The GUARD unlocks the door and descends to get Bruno. The
INQUISITORS rustle their papers and confer briefly, until the shock
of BRUNO's entrance silences them. Physically, he is a twisted man.
The GUARD has to support him. In spite of this, as he sits, he still
manages a flash of the old humour.*

BRUNO: Excuse me my decrepitude, good sirs!
Your ministers below were over zealous!

*They have the grace to be ashamed for the moment. The PRIOR
makes another small show of strength.*

PRIOR GABRIELLI (*to guard*): Bring cordial and a goblet. Set it by
His chair!

The GUARD goes out.

PRIOLI: Are you well enough to stand
A questioning?

BRUNO (*quiet*): I do not know. At least
I am less pained than on the rack!

PRIOR GABRIELLI: I read a text. You wrote it in your book –
'The Cause, the Principle, the One': You speak
Of this Elizabeth of England, who
Usurped the throne, murdered the rightful heir
And blasphemously nominates herself
Head of the Church, Protector of the Faith!

(*He quotes with extra emphasis.*)

'I praise her, the Divine Elizabeth,
A queen in title and in dignity,
Whose presence sheds bright light on all the world,
Whom no prince can excel in knowledge, art
Or generosity.' The words are yours?

BRUNO: They are.

PRIOR GABRIELLI: The lady is a heretic?

BRUNO: Yes.

PRIOR GABRIELLI: A persecutor of the Church?

BRUNO: Yes!

PRIOR GABRIELLI: And yet to her, you dare apply,
A title which belongs to God alone:
'Divine'!

*BRUNO gets a diversion at this moment as the GUARD brings
in the cordial and goblet and a tabouret. He sets them up beside
Bruno. BRUNO awkwardly tries to pour a drink.*

MOROSINI *(to guard)*: Help him, man! For God's sake, help!

*The GUARD pours liquor for Bruno. He drinks and hands back
the cup. He has had time to collect himself. MOROSINI watches him
carefully. His reaction is crucial for Morosini.*

BRUNO *(very carefully)*: My lords, in this I do admit to
error.
I should not have praised a heretic.
But, consider this in mitigation.
I was much at court – her court! – a guest
Of the Ambassador of France. I hope
You will not make a courtly compliment
A test of orthodoxy!

They give him a slight chuckle for this one. He goes on.

                              The epithet
'Divine'? This is the fashion and convention
In a woman's court. A brooch, a ring,
A ribbon or a wig – all are divine!
The Queen herself can hardly merit less!

There is another chuckle, but TAVERNA stifles it swiftly.

TAVERNA: Good Brother Bruno, it would seem you were
  More courtier than Christian.
BRUNO (*humbly*): Yes, I was,
  And I regret it.
TAVERNA: Pause a moment, Brother!
  You know – none better – in the early Church
  The test of faith was to refuse to name
  The Emperor 'divine'.
BRUNO: It was not made
  A test in London. Besides, my faith was known
  And never abdicated.
TAVERNA: Which was your faith
  When you dined out with one Sir Philip Sidney,
  To whom you dedicated this – (*he waves the volume*) – this
    foul
  And monstrous fable, 'The Triumphant Beast'
  To satirize the Holy Father?
    BRUNO, *in his weakened state, cannot stand up to the virulence
  of the attack. He drifts a moment vaguely, like a stunned fighter.*
BRUNO: My faith . . . ?
  Faith is . . .
    He slumps in his chair.
TAVERNA: Answer, man!
PRIOR GABRIELLI (*sudden eruption*): I will not
  Endure this tyranny! Nuncio or not,
  You are still bound to simple justice. This,
  After the rack, is butchery!
TAVERNA (*sinister and cold*): Prior,
  You forget yourself:
PRIOR GABRIELLI (*ignores him*): Eminence!
  I call on you, the Shepherd of the Sheep,
  – The lost ones too! Messer Morosini,
  Assessor for the State, you witness this!
MOROSINI: Recorder, set it down! Justice is mocked
  If this continues!

PRIOLI (*the diplomat*): See to Brother Bruno!

    The GUARD *and the* RECORDER *go to him, they give him cordial, bathe his forehead, etc.*

PRIOLI (*to Taverna*): Not long since we reproved a witness here
  For lack of charity. I would not see,
  The Pope, my master shamed for the same fault
  In you.

    TAVERNA *is too canny to fight back. He bows acknowledgement.*

TAVERNA: I beg an absolution for
  My zealotry!

MOROSINI (*bland*): We are your colleagues, tell us.
  What do you want from Bruno?

TAVERNA: Do we not
  All want the same thing. Admission of error,
  Rejection of false doctrine, penance and
  Reform . . .

PRIOLI: If he offers that, then we,
  Good shepherds, take him back into the fold.

MOROSINI: Ask him!

    All turn to BRUNO, *who is recovering, and who still manages the graveyard humour.*

BRUNO: Strange! I felt a sudden slip,
  Towards the edge of time. You almost lost me.

TAVERNA (*calmly*): Giordano Bruno, are you an honest man?

BRUNO (*a tired grin*): By and large I am. Sometimes more by
  And sometimes larger. Still, I think at core
  I'm honest.

TAVERNA: So we ask you, having a care
  For your sick body and your troubled soul,
  Will you recant your errors?

    BRUNO *considers the question and summons his strength for a shrewd answer.*

BRUNO: In general?
  Or in particular?

TAVERNA: Why do you ask?

BRUNO (*summoning his fading strength*): Because, in general, and
   truthfully,
   I can admit to errors – many of them!
   But pin me to particulars – without
   A text, or strength for argument, I could
   Admit monstrosities. I will not do it.
TAVERNA: Would you, in a penitential time,
   – And penance would be asked, but clemency
   Extended – would you, in sober solitude
   Examine all your texts, confer, reflect
   And finally recant what might be shown
   False to the Apostolic Doctrine?
      BRUNO *reflects again. He is very tired now.*
BRUNO: Yes.
   I would promise that, but not without
   The scholar's right of argument.
TAVERNA: Who
   Would deny it? (*To tribunal.*) I am satisfied for now!
      There is a murmur of agreement round the table.
PRIOLI: Approach the table, Brother.
      BRUNO *rises with difficulty. He has to be helped by the guard.*
   Kneel!
      Supporting himself on the table, BRUNO *kneels painfully.*
   There is
   No formulary. Express yourself as if
   To God.
      BRUNO *closes his eyes, gathers himself and then staggers through
   his recantation.*
BRUNO: My lords, I have, with all sincerity,
   Searched heart and conscience and I know that I
   Have given cause for scandal and suspicion.
   I am ready to reform my life,
   Repair the scandal, reject the heresies
   I have or may have entertained,
   And which I now abhor. (*He begins to break.*) For these my sins,

I ask a humble pardon of my God,
Of you, my brethren and superiors,
I willingly accept the punishment
You will determine for me. And I beg ...
I beg ... I ...

He breaks and cradles his head on the table, weeping uncontrollably.

PRIOLI (*a ritual question*): Have you anything else to say?

Slowly, BRUNO *raises his head and looks at him with terrible pathos.*

BRUNO: No.
There is nothing else!

PRIOLI makes a sign to the guard, who leads BRUNO *like a sleepwalker to his cell. Then* TAVERNA *springs his trap.*

TAVERNA: A pretty scene!
But Rome will not be satisfied. I serve
A notice on the Church of Venice and the State,
The Holy Office will ask for extradition
Of this notorious heresiarch
For further process of this case!

MOROSINI (*checkmated and shocked*): You dare not
Do this!

TAVERNA: I do nothing, sir. I am
A Papal messenger! And you but serve
As state assessor. Let our masters fight
The battle, eh? – This is a traders' town,
They'll come to terms! – Eminence, goodday.

He bows and exits, the only victor of the day. The others stare after him.

CURTAIN

ACT THREE

SCENE ONE

Rome. *Seven years later. Bruno's cell in the Prison of the Inquisition.*
The cell is furnished with a pallet bed, a table and chair, a stool, in the
corner a wooden bucket. On the table there is a single candlestick,
quills and ink, a pile of parchment.

It is just dawn, a grey light enters from a barred window just at
eye-level. The candle is guttering out. BRUNO, *who has worked*
a great part of the night, is sleeping at the table, head buried on his
arms.

He is seven years older. His hair is greying. He is seamed and scored by
his years of confinement. He limps a little as a consequence of his
tortures. But throughout this final act, there is a strange, remote calm
about him.

There is a rattle of bolts on the cell door. BRUNO *stirs and wakes*
painfully. The door opens. A GAOLER *enters with Bruno's breakfast,*
a cup of water, bread, a bowl of meal, a spoon. He sets it glumly on
the table. Then he crosses to pick up the toilet bucket.

BRUNO *surveys the breakfast with distaste. He bounces the hard loaf on*
the table.

BRUNO (*grins*): When do they bake fresh bread?

GAOLER: Every seven years!

BRUNO: That gives me hope!
I have been here longer than the loaves. (*He tastes the meal.*)
It's cold!

GAOLER: Be glad you're listed with a charity!
Else you'd be eating slops three times a day!

    BRUNO *chuckles. The* GAOLER *goes out, closing the door.*

BRUNO *notices the guttering candle. He blows it out. He makes a half-hearted effort to eat the meal, dipping the bread into his mug. Then he pushes it away.*

He crumbles some of the bread in his hands, crosses to the window, stands on the stool and looks out. He whistles a bird-call and scatters the crumbs on the window-ledge. He whistles again. No birds come.

BRUNO: Where are you, little bird? Have you forgotten
 Brother Bruno? I wish the others would
 Forget him, too. They won't. In Rome, the stones
 Remember!

  (*He whistles again, then shivers.*)
 When will spring be here? Please,
 Fly me a little sun from Africa!
 I'm cold.

 He climbs down stiffly from his stool and returns to the table. He picks up a large official document and scans it wearily.
 A petition from Giordano Bruno,
 Prisoner, unto his Sanctity Pope Clement
 Felicitously reigning ... Boh! Rejected!

 He tosses the document down on the table, moves to the bed and flings himself down in utter weariness. He lies staring at the ceiling, talking to himself.
 Bruno, they have you penned – a silly sheep,
 Fly-blown and draggle-tailed. There's no way out
 Save through the little gate and down the chute
 Into the douche box, where they wash you clean,
 Before you join the other happy lambs
 In God's green pastures. Is that what you want?
 You have it. Just a signature
 On Master Bellarmino's document,
 A day of public penance in a church,
 And you'll be free ... Free for what? And who
 Then will you be? A cherub with pink cheeks,
 A little brainless smile, no body and

G

A pair of winglets sprouting at the neck?
O God! How they interpret your once grand
Design! . . .

Again there is a rattle of bolts, the door opens and the BARBER
*enters. He is a cheery, elderly, talkative fellow, with his bowl and
kettle and towel and little bag of instruments. His visit is unexpected.*
BRUNO *is delighted to see him. He gets up to greet him.*

BRUNO: Sir Barber! Knight of the shears and razor!

BARBER (*playing a familiar comedy*): Your Eminence! A benedic-
    tion, please!

BRUNO: God keep your razor sharp, my son and steady!

BARBER: Amen!

The BARBER *makes a bustle of laying out his tools.*

BRUNO: What brings you here today?

BARBER (*points piously upwards*): Orders
    From heaven.

BRUNO: Oh-oh! That's ominous!

The BARBER *kicks the cell door shut and then rummages furtively
in his bag.*

BARBER: I brought
    A little something. This!

He holds up an orange.

BRUNO (*delighted*): Oh no!

BARBER: My son
    Delivered me a pannier full.

*BRUNO *handles the orange as though it were gold. The* BARBER
is delighted. He fishes again.

BARBER: And these!

He holds up a posy of violets. BRUNO *is hard put to restrain his
tears. He puts down the orange and takes the flowers eagerly.*

BRUNO: Winter violets . . .

BARBER: My little niece
    Picked them this morning in the Field of Flowers.

BRUNO (*caught in a sudden memory*): 'My dear, dear friend, so
    much a cloudwalker,

You do not see the violets in the grass ... '
The BARBER *is embarrassed by the emotion.*
BARBER: They need fresh water!
BRUNO (*recovers*): That we have, my friend!
  He takes his mug, puts the violets in it and sets it on the window-ledge.
There! They'll share my little light, and I
Will breathe their perfume. Now, Sir Barber, make
Giordano Bruno look like a cardinal!
  He seats himself, the BARBER *goes through all the flourishes of making him ready. He studies him like an artist's model, then begins to clip and talk.*
BARBER: What shall it be? A tonsure? No, I think
  A dash of gallantry ... We used to have
  A fine bright company of cardinals –
  Not virtuous, mind, but very colourful,
  Plumed hats, slashed hose and crimson velvet cloaks.
  ... Now they're all saints, or if they're not, they're wise
  And keep their follies off the streets. It's now
  The Jesuits who set the pace! Smart fellows,
  Sharp as rapiers, and disciplined ...
BRUNO: I know. I have their Robert Bellarmino
  Writing me lovenotes while he cuts me up.
  A barber-surgeon for their Holy Office!
BARBER: Why do you fight them? You are getting grey!
  You're thin on top! Soon I'll be clipping peach bloom!
  Why don't you give them what they want and quit.
  Go back to Naples and the sun! There's heart
  And music there! We Romans are a stiff
  And stubborn bunch – bad haters, too!
BRUNO (*grins*): Good Sir Knight, just trim my hair and beard!
BARBER: Mamma! All Southerners have wooden heads!
BRUNO (*chuckles*): Now that's a truth!
BARBER: Don't move, I'll chop your ears.
  You know the Field of Flowers?

BRUNO: No.

BARBER: That's
  Where the violets come from.

BRUNO: Oh!

BARBER: Also,
  That's where they burn you at the stake, my friend!

BRUNO: Better the violets, eh?

BARBER: You've never seen
  A burning?

BRUNO: Nor baited bears, nor killed a bull!

BARBER: Now for the beard. Head back ... It's quite a day,
  To buy a place in front costs gold!

BRUNO: Indeed!

BARBER: Better than Carnival! The whole town's out,
  There's a procession, see, from Nona Tower
  To the Campo. The fellow for the stake,
  He rides an ass. There's guards and pikemen and
  A trumpeter. Then there's the Company
  Of Mercy – they have a better name, St. John-
  Who-lost-his-head! They carry relics,
  Pictures, crucifixes, so if you want
  A final absolution at the stake,
  They give it. If you don't, the guards will twist
  Your arms and make you seem to kiss the cross.
  If you're obstreperous and make a shout,
  They tie your tongue ... ugh!

BRUNO: That's enough!
  Just ply the scissors!

BARBER (realizing): God! I am a fool.

BRUNO (gently): No! You tell a lively tale! I wonder
  How it will read five hundred years from now?
  – To make a man confess a loving God
  You burn him!

BARBER: You'll never burn! There's too much sap
  In you!

(*He ends his work with a flourish, whips off the towel.*)
There now! His Eminence is served!
A mirror!

BRUNO surveys himself in the mirror.

BRUNO: Good! I could even meet the Pope,
Provided he would come.

The BARBER is packing his things. BRUNO crosses to him and takes him by the shoulders.

Knight of the Shears,
I cannot pay you. But from my deepest heart,
Thanks for the few hours of liberty
I've known.

The BARBER, deeply moved, takes his hand and kisses it.

BARBER: Each time I've come, there has been pain
For you.

BRUNO (*very serious*): I tell you something, friend, when I
First came to Rome, I was a nothing man.
In Venice they had me weeping on my knees
Begging for pity. I've wept here, too – but that's
A different kind of tears. I've begged here, too
For respite from the torturers. But deep
Inside, a new bud of a man began
To grow – and *you*, my little barber, were
The gardener, you with your clicking scissors,
Clacking tongue, your gifts of laughter and
Your violets, your plums and oranges.
You gave me back my dignity.

BARBER: God keep you!

He gathers his things awkwardly and hurries out. BRUNO stands a moment, deep in thought, then goes to the window, gets down the violets and holds them in his cupped hands, contemplating them.

BRUNO: Christ! What a choice to make. To smell the violets
Or the faggot-pile! To walk each day
In the green countryside, to feel the rain

Upon my face, chew on a wheat-stalk,
Watch the tender shoots of next year's grapes,
Curl around the vine-poles, and the poplar trees.
– Or else, to make that long, last donkey-ride
Between the pikemen to the stake, to hear
The shouting, and the chant of hypocrites,
To be a spectacle for animals
In human masks!

He stiffens in agony, holding the violets as if they are a pillar to support him. The door creaks open and clicks shut, and he turns sharply to see PRIOR GABRIELLI *standing against the door. The Prior has aged too. He is subdued and humble, and yet has increased in dignity.*

PRIOR GABRIELLI: Brother Bruno.

BRUNO (*holding himself to formality*): Prior!

PRIOR GABRIELLI (*embarrassed*): Violets! They're blooming in our garden too.

BRUNO (*a touch of irony*): My barber brought me these.

PRIOR GABRIELLI: May we talk?

BRUNO (*weary refusal*): I fear I have spent all my words. I've had
Inquisitors, assessors, counsellors,
Our Master-General, a confessor,
Four advocates and various visitors,
Augustinians and Jesuits,
Friars Discalced and Friars Capuchin,
Persuading me to flee the fire and join
The company of the elect. I crave
A little peace.

PRIOR GABRIELLI: I come, a private man.

BRUNO hesitates a moment and then points to the chair.

BRUNO: Please, sit down.

The PRIOR *seats himself behind the table.* BRUNO *perches on the corner of it, begins to juggle the orange and then peel it.*

PRIOR GABRIELLI: I was the man who gave
To Mocenigo, the notion of betrayal.

BRUNO (*ignores the admission*): How is my lady?

PRIOR GABRIELLI: Well, and yet, not well.
There is no loving in that house, and you –
The memory of what was done to you –
Haunts every hallway.

BRUNO: Tell her from me – tell her –
What little calm I have, she gave. What grace
I find in this so graceless world, is hers.

PRIOR GABRIELLI: I promise that.

BRUNO: Taverna, Morosini,
Mocenigo?

PRIOR GABRIELLI: These are straw men, blown
By every wind of power.

BRUNO: I clutch at straws,
A man in a wild river crying 'help'
– And no one hears!

PRIOR GABRIELLI (*hesitant*): Bruno!

BRUNO: Yes.

PRIOR GABRIELLI: To say I pity you would be a slight
Upon us both. Never in all my life
Have I known such a man. I hate what you
Profess. You, I admire as being more –
Much more – a man, and more believer, too
Than half the canting orthodox. But Bruno,
You are such a numbskull! A billy-goat,
Butting his head against the bastions
Of Castel Angelo. That's the Pope's
Own fortress. Who must win, the billy-goat
Or the Pope?

    BRUNO *grins and pops a slice of orange into his mouth.*

BRUNO: A billy-goat! Now there's a name for Bruno!

PRIOR GABRIELLI: And have you ever found a name
For me?

BRUNO (*a moment's reflection*): Yes. I think I have. You are
A man who has a talent for belief.

You're fortunate. Give you good premises,
You'll draw a safe conclusion. Then you pull
The shutters down and say: 'The light is plenty
For the road to Paradise.' Hand you
A torch, you'll set the world on fire and call it
Christendom, no matter who gets burned.

PRIOR GABRIELLI: Not bad! And yet I envy you, and you
I think, do sometimes envy me!

    BRUNO *hands him a piece of orange. He accepts it.*

BRUNO: I do.

That's a good orange. My first since God knows when!

PRIOR GABRIELLI (*munching*): I disapprove of all this cruelty.

BRUNO (*attacks*): And yet – so the Pope puts his name to it,
Or, with a God-like gesture shrugs it off
On to the civil state – you will accept
The last brutality?

PRIOR GABRIELLI: If I do not,
Who tells me then, good Bruno, right and wrong?

BRUNO: Is it necessary?

PRIOR GABRIELLI: Yes! How else
Can we comport ourselves as Christian men?

BRUNO: Look at the document before you.

    The PRIOR *picks up the parchment and scans it.*

PRIOR GABRIELLI: I saw it
At the Holy Office.

BRUNO: Those are eight
Separate propositions from my books
Declared heretical.

PRIOR GABRIELLI: In fact, they are.

BRUNO: Who says so?

PRIOR GABRIELLI: Bellarmino and the best
Of all our theologians.

BRUNO: Honest men,
I have no doubt of it. But tell me, Prior,

Who says God whispers in their ears. Who says
That Bellarmino is infallible?
PRIOR GABRIELLI: The Pope accepts his verdict.
BRUNO: But the Pope
  Has never read a single line of all
  My treatises. How can he judge the frame
  In which I speak? Even the language!
  I'm a Nolan. I could dazzle you
  In dialect, because the words do not
  Make the same sense to different men. Our Popes
  – Now tell me honestly – have they
  The gift of tongues?
PRIOR GABRIELLI (*wry*): God help us! No!
BRUNO: Now here's the terror of it! Here are you
  And here am I, munching a juicy orange.
  Am I a devil with a pitchfork tail?
PRIOR GABRIELLI: No!
BRUNO: Could you believe that I might be
  In purest conscience before God – if not
  The Church?
PRIOR GABRIELLI: I could.
BRUNO: And could you, as they propose,
  For that clear conscience – kill me?
PRIOR GABRIELLI: Never! No!
BRUNO: Suppose I kneel now and say to you,
  Good Prior, there may be doubts, but I have none,
  Give me the sacrament, absolve me from
  My sins. What will you do, as confessor?
PRIOR GABRIELLI: I will absolve you in the same good
    faith.
BRUNO: And I'll accept the absolution – if
  You'll walk tomorrow to the stake with me!
    The PRIOR *is deeply shocked.*
PRIOR GABRIELLI: To make what affirmation?
BRUNO: Only this!

To shout abroad that God Almighty made
Of every man a self. This was the first
Gift and the last. And we, to hold that gift
Safe for our brothers and our sons – must die!
There is a long pause. The PRIOR *holds up the document.*

PRIOR GABRIELLI: What have you done with this?

BRUNO: Nothing – yet!

PRIOR GABRIELLI: Then sign while there is time. They want
    you free!
You are a shame to them. Accept the key.
Walk out into the daylight and forget
The sad and sterile years of argument.

BRUNO (*very quiet*): I, too, want to be free. I have not seen
The sun for seven years. I have – by Christ –
Made test of every compromise by which
I still might sign and keep a single shred
Of self-hood. – And they come this very day
To ask my answer.

PRIOR GABRIELLI: Give them 'no', my friend,
And you are dead!

BRUNO: It is not death I fear.
Already I have died a dozen deaths,
Waiting for torture and the questioning.
The terror that haunts me is quite different:
To see and know on that last Calvary,
The ultimate malice of inventive man! (*A terrible summation.*)
They will make me a clown before I die.
The PRIOR *agrees. He gropes for a word of consolation. He finds
a paradox.*

PRIOR GABRIELLI: Christ died a clown! – A cardboard king,
    his crown
A twist of briar thorns!

BRUNO (*muses on it*): Perhaps he was.
Perhaps that is the truth of it, that man
And only man can mock himself – and mock

The artifacts he calls divinities.

There is a pause.

PRIOR GABRIELLI: If you wish, I'll bear you company
Until they come.

BRUNO (*touched*): Prior, my thanks, but truly,
I am a braver man alone, without
An audience for my loose and braggart tongue.

*The PRIOR gets up heavily, crosses to Bruno. Then he fishes in
his habit and brings out his breviary. He hands it to Bruno. BRUNO
accepts it.*

PRIOR GABRIELLI: If you would like to pray, this is my
book.

BRUNO (*moved and savage*): I do not wish to pray. Be there a God,
He has a debt to me and, being just,
Will pay it. If there be no God, (*A real agony*)
No prayer, no incantation will assuage
The monstrous agony of human kind. (*Relaxes.*)
But I will keep the book for brotherhood.

*There is the sound of measured footfalls. They both turn. Three
Curial OFFICIALS and two armed GUARDS enter the cell. One of
the officials is a Notary. He carries a rolled document.*

NOTARY: Giordano Bruno?

BRUNO: Myself.

NOTARY: I am required
To put a question.

BRUNO (*controlled*): I know the question, sir.
I need a moment's quiet.

*The NOTARY bows assent. BRUNO turns away and moves to the
window. He bows his head, puts hands to forehead to still the beating
inside his skull. After a long moment he turns, haggard but chal-
lenging.*

BRUNO: Let us be clear!
This is what you ask: 'Rejoin the flock,
Recite the Creeds. Deny what once you wrote
Believing it was true. Then make an act

Of public penitence – we'll let you live!
Refuse, we kill you!' That's the nub of it!

   No one challenges his interpretation. After a long pause, he goes on quietly.

Which of you gentlemen begot me? Which
Breathed into this sack of bones, the life
I did not ask for? None of you? Who then?
Aldobrandini, who is now the Pope?
Did Bellarmino? Any Cardinal
Of the Inquisitors? Who said to me,
A foetus in the womb, a puking babe,
'You have your life, but on the condition that
You thus believe?' – No one! Not even God!
So, gentlemen, I say you have no right,
To make terms for my life. I tell you then –
No! I will not recant. I will not sign!

   The NOTARY *simply nods, unrolls his parchment and begins to read. The sentence which he reads is the actual one passed upon Giordano Bruno, and must be delivered in such a fashion as to watch, but be different from the blank verse of the rest of the play. It must convey by its very legalism the enormity of Bruno's fate.*

NOTARY: Having invoked the name of our Lord Jesus Christ
   And of his most Glorious Mother Mary ever Virgin
   In the cause of the aforesaid causes
   Brought before this Holy Office
   Between, on the one hand
   The procurator Fiscal of the said Holy Office,
   And on the other hand, yourself,
   The aforesaid Giordano Bruno the accused,
   Examined, brought to trial
   And found guilty, impenitent,
   Obstinate and pertinacious,
   In this, our sentence,
   Determined by the counsel and opinion of our advisers,

The Reverend Fathers,
Masters in Sacred Theology and Doctors in both laws,
We hereby, in these documents,
Publish, announce, pronounce, sentence,
And declare you, Brother Giordano Bruno,
To be an impenitent heretic,
And therefore to have incurred
All the ecclesiastical censures
And pains of the Holy Canon,
The laws and the constitutions,
Both general and particular,
Imposed on such
Confessed impenitent, pertinacious
And obstinate heretics,
Wherefore as such we verbally degrade you
And declare that you must be degraded,
And we hereby ordain and command
That you shall be actually degraded
From all your ecclesiastical orders
Both major and minor
In which you have been ordained,
According to the Sacred Canon Law;
And that you must be driven forth,
And we do drive you forth
From our ecclesiastical forum
And from our Holy and Immaculate Church
Of whose mercy you have become unworthy.
And we ordain and command
That you must be delivered to the Secular Court
    (*He pronounces the terrible and hypocritical irony.*)
That you may be punished
With the punishment deserved,
Though we earnestly pray
That it will mitigate the
Rigor of the laws

Concerning the pains of your person,
That you may not be in danger of death
Or of mutilation of your members.
Furthermore, we condemn,
We reprobate and we prohibit
All your aforesaid and your other books and writings
As heretical and erroneous,
Containing many heresies and errors,
And we ordain that all of them
Which have come or may in future come
Into the hands of the Holy Office
Shall be publicly destroyed and burned
Upon the Square of St. Peter,
Before the steps,
And that they shall be placed
On the Index of Forbidden Books.
And as we have commanded, so shall it be done.
And thus we say, pronounce, sentence, declare,
Degrade, command and ordain,
We chase forth and deliver
And we pray in this
And every other better method and form
That we reasonably can and should.
Thus pronounce we,
The Cardinal General Inquisitors,
Whose names subscribe this document.
    The NOTARY *rolls up his parchment.*
From this moment, you are, as to your body,
At the disposal of the Secular Court.
As to your soul, may God have mercy on you.
    BRUNO *digests the terrible words and then nods slowly.*
BRUNO: At this moment, gentlemen, I think
That you are more afraid of me, than I
Of you.
    Then, with the old monastic gesture of retirement, he pulls his

cowl up over his face, and stands, holding the book, in the attitude of the statue in the Campo dei Fiori.

The others withdraw and leave him alone.

The lights change. As they do, he seems to turn into stone, a defiant figure, permanently accusing tyranny.

THE CURTAIN FALLS